How To
Find, Build, Rent and
Sell Billboards
For Big Profits

Written by **Frank Rolfe**

January 25, 2007

The information provided in this book is intended to be a general guideline and not the ultimate source of information. When appropriate, you should consult your own legal, accounting, financial, and other advice.

ISBN 978-0-6151-6905-7

Table of Contents

Biography

Frank Rolfe started his billboard empire from his coffee table, as a fresh graduate from Stanford University. It began as a resume builder for graduate school applications, and ended with a sale to a public company 14 years later.

Using unique strategies he developed from desperate competition with much larger adversaries, Rolfe eventually owned more billboard units than any private individual in Dallas/Ft. Worth. Along the way, he fine-tuned the techniques to find billboard locations, rent advertising space, and sell signs and leases.

Rolfe was an aggressive buyer of billboards during the Texas recession of 1988-1992, and built or bought during his career the astounding average of two billboard faces per month – one every two weeks for fourteen years straight. He was also able to individually rent one billboard face every two days.

Rolfe currently owns and operates mobile home parks, and lives with his wife and daughter in a small town in the Midwest.

Introduction

In 1982, armed with only a desire to make lots of money, I began a 14 year odyssey to build a full-scale billboard company. I had no training or mentors – nothing. Everything you read in this book I learned the hard way, through countless mistakes, missed opportunities and embarrassment.

There were 60 billboard companies in Dallas when I began. The competition was impossible. But I hung in there when others gave up; I developed special niches that I worked aggressively. When I sold out at the end of 1996, I had become the largest private owner of billboards (based on number of units) in Dallas/Ft. Worth. About 70% of the billboards I had built from scratch, and another 30% I had purchased.

Everything you are about to read worked for me, and should work for you. Every market is different, the economy goes up and down, but some basics remain intact no matter where you start at. When you find those niches that work for you, drive a freight train through them – give it 100% of your focus until it stops working. Most billboard companies got their start from a lucky niche – a landowner with multiple locations, a new highway being built, a change in laws that suddenly allows new billboards to be built. But always remember that you make your own luck. The more you try, the more likely it is that you will get a break.

Always remember Teddy Roosevelt's quote, "The only people who never make mistakes are those who never do anything". There is never a reason for embarrassment for trying something out. The high value of billboards today makes it an extremely lucrative hobby if it never develops into a full time job. One good billboard lease can buy you a house. Until you build the structure, the actual financial risk and investment is nearly zero.

Understanding
What Creates Value

Limited supply, I had an economics degree from Stanford, and the main thing I remembered was the concept of supply and demand. An industry built on a limited supply of a product, coupled with a growing demand, is always a winner. And such is the billboard industry. Laws keep dwindling the supply of new locations to build. It's this scarcity that creates value. Don't get upset when you have trouble finding legal billboard locations initially—that scarcity is what makes it worth doing. Before there were tough billboard laws, billboards weren't worth anything. Anybody could build a billboard anywhere they wanted to at any time. If an advertiser needed a billboard they could just build their own. Things were so worthless that advertisers sometimes paid the landowner with their product – a big can of motor oil was the groundrent for Amalie billboards in the old days. Nobody could make any money in that environment, except the sign painters and fabricators. Ladybird Johnson, who introduced the Highway Beautification Act, is really the unwitting mother of the modern billboard industry. Without her, big billboards, big rents and big values wouldn't exist.

Location, location, location if this is the catch phrase for real estate, then it also holds true for billboards. Any idiot can build a big billboard in the middle of nowhere. The key is to find desirable locations that advertisers will want to rent. As you'll see, often that seems impossible. Many times, you will have to build a billboard a bit out of the mainstream and wait for the market to mature. I always found the key question was, "Can I rent this sign for enough to cover the bills until the market gets bigger?"

Visibility is the third key driver to creating value. A location that is desirable is worthless if you can't see it. And don't kid yourself with the marginal location that you can only see if you crane your neck after the bridge overpass – advertisers just aren't that dumb.

If you look for good billboard locations for a while and fail – rejoice. That means that when you do find one it will be worth a lot of money. A market with plentiful locations is what really worries me.

Getting Started

O.K., you want to go ahead. The first question you have to answer is "What market?" I define a market as a geographic location that has a set of billboard ordinances in place. A good market will have some or all of the following criteria:

- Legal locations to build (an ordinance that allows for new construction)

- High traffic roads (advertisers want a lot of eyes seeing their billboards)

- Large volume of potential advertisers (a lot of businesses in the area)

- Low ground rents to landowners (the industry shoots for 15% to 20% of revenue)

- High advertising rates

- Few billboard competitors

What if my hometown doesn't have these dynamics?

Then you have to drive a bit to one that does. My normal territory extended up to three hours from my house. Billboard management is not that time intensive, so managing a distant market is O.K.

Fly out of town? I've done it. I managed some billboards we bought in Los Angeles for five years. You have to have a big enough core of billboards to make the numbers work, however.

Once a market proves to not be that good, just move on. Anywhere you live in America; there must be fifty markets to look at.

Checking the laws

Most markets have both state and city laws regarding billboards.

The state laws are normally handled by the Highway Department. Call the Highway Department and get a copy of the billboard laws for you to read. They are pretty clear cut, and normally include illustrations.

If the state allows new billboards, then contact the city hall of the market you are looking at, and get a copy of their laws. <u>Never</u> ask the city person what the laws are. They will always lie and tell you that they don't allow new billboards. Billboards are something that most towns do not want to encourage.

Once you get the billboard ordinance, highlight all the areas that pertain to building billboards, such as zonings, spacing, etc. Don't confuse the sections on premise signs (business signs such as Wendy's and McDonalds) and non-premise signs, which are billboards. If the ordinance allows for the building of new billboards, then you are ready to move to the next step.

Doing more market research

Most state highway departments have what is called a highway traffic count map. Some are free, some you have to purchase. It is basically a map that shows a series of lines representing highways and numbers every inch or so. It shows how many cars pass by that spot in a 24 hour period. Normally, this is the traffic going both ways, so an advertiser would be reaching about 50% of this number. The important thing is that these numbers be big. How big? I would say at least 5,000 vehicles per day on a non-highway street, and about 20,000 on a highway. Some highways in big cities can reach over 250,000 vehicles per day. This is one case in which bigger is <u>always</u> better.

To check the number of advertisers in the market, get a copy of the yellow pages. If it's thick, with a lot of advertisers, good news. If it's skinny, you need to watch out. You can also drive the roads and see if you see alot of businesses.

To get the average groundrent, call some businesses that have billboards on their property, and ask them how much the billboard company is paying them. You will be amazed at how much information these people will freely give you. Then call a billboard company and ask them what they will pay you for a hypothetical billboard location. Again, they will usually tell you everything you need to know.

To check advertising rates, follow the same procedure. Call the sales guy at a big billboard company and ask him what he charges to advertise. They will often send you a whole kit, free of charge, which shows all of their ad rates in the entire market. Or call the phone number on a blank billboard and ask them, "How much?" The data is easy to obtain.

To find the other billboard companies in the market, again refer to the yellow pages. The billboard companies are normally under "Advertising – Outdoor" or "Advertising – Other". A good market would have maybe five companies. Be sure to exclude the non-billboard listings such as "balloon advertising", etc. There is also a nationwide directory of Outdoor Advertising companies on OutdoorBillboard.com under the heading of Outdoor Advertising From A-Z.

Tools you will need

So you've found a market you like. Now it is time to gather your weapons and ammo. First, you need a "virtual identity". No one is going to sign a billboard ground lease with you if you do not appear legitimate. Fortunately, the advent of voice mail, cell phones, email, and desktop publishing has leveled the playing field between big companies and start ups. Early on in my career, I made a proposal along with several other huge companies. At the time, I had maybe three billboards. I took great photographs, cut and pasted maps – a lot of work went into my presentation. A couple of weeks later I got the call that I had won the bidding. Astonished, I asked why they chose me. They said, "You were less money, but they really wanted the security of a big company like yours." Because of my extra effort, they thought I, with three billboards, was bigger than my competitors who had three hundred.

A good setup would be a nice business card and letterhead tied to a P.O. Box, with a cell number and email. You will also need a catchy name – something that sounds "big company". Billboard companies normally are one word, which is shown on the billboard itself, underneath the ad. Popular names from the past include 3M, Whiteco, Lamar, Van Wagner, etc. Choose a name; if possible, that implies a tie in to a household name. For example, my company name was Chase. When I called someone and said I was with Chase, they would often think Chase Manhattan Bank and take the call.

Obviously, you will need a cell phone and email accessibility. A fax line would help to, particularly when you start processing contracts.

Several other specialized tools you will need:

- Zoning Map of your Market. This shows you the zoning of all the property that fronts the highway or road. Take your billboard ordinance and find the section in zonings that allow for billboards. Now highlight areas of the legal zonings that front your desired highway or road.

- A camera. Landowners love to see photos of their property, to show where the billboard would go. Digital is probably best.

- A magnetic sign to put on the car door of your auto, made up of the name of your company inside a rectangle or oval. Always, put it on only when meeting a landowner in the field to look like a big company. Immediately remove it once you leave, since you do not want to tip off a competitor that you were there.

- A measuring device that is sometimes called a "Rollawheel." Basically, it is a bicycle tire that measures distance in feet as you push it with a handle. You can buy the basic model at Home Depot, and the fancy one at a surveying equipment store. This device will soon be your best buddy, as you are about to walk miles and miles together.

- Aerial photos. These make identifying the potential site much easier on zoning and ownership maps, because surrounding landmarks act as a "guide" on the spot.

Looking for Locations

Now that you have knowledge of the billboard ordinances, a color-coded zoning map and your measuring wheel, it's time to hit the streets in search of a billboard location. It's a very low-tech process. You start at the very first property that is properly zoned for billboards in your market, and start measuring with your odometer if there is a potential location with sufficient spacing down the street that is also in the correct zoning. Remember that your odometer on your car reads 528' (feet) = 1 tenth. If the required spacing is 1,500' (feet) between billboards, then you would need 3/10 of a mile on your odometer to equal a potential site from the nearest billboard. If you happen upon a legally zoned site with the correct spacing on your odometer, it's time to get out your measuring wheel and start really getting a handle on the measurement. Unfortunately, the odometer test is often wrong. Once you get out of your car and start accurately measuring, you may find a discrepancy of 100' (feet) or more. If the spacing is not there, just immediately drive on to the next location. There are no clever ways around the math of spacing or zonings. Once you find a location that truly has the correct spacing and zoning, you need to catalog everything you can about this site, and even photograph it to refresh your memory. Write down any street address you see, if there is a business on it and what its name is, even a landmark of another business across the street or next door. This will come in very handy when you move to the property owner search part of your assignment. This whole process sounds complicated, but after a while, it becomes absolute routine. In a world of video games, this difficulty level is about like "Pong", the very first game ever. The most awkward part of the process is handling the oversized zoning maps in your front seat. It is essential, for safe driving, that you pull over and park when consulting the maps. Don't be in a rush, as it is essential that you competently research every inch of your market.

Finding the owner

Once you have a few sites that you are interested in, its time to head for the property tax records of your market. This is often entitled the (your city) Appraisal District. Once you get there, try and find someone who can help you and show you how to work the system. Some cities are computerized in their property tax records, and some are not. It is very hard to know what you are doing the first time out, so don't be shy about getting help. Don't tell them you are looking for billboard sites – everyone hates billboards and then they will not be helpful. Tell them you are looking at a piece of land to buy. Often, the sites you will be trying to identify will be pieces of raw land without any structures or addresses. These are particularly hard to locate in property tax records, because there are no street addresses or landmarks to work from. You may have to use aerial maps to try and locate the exact property you want, and that's when those landmarks on neighboring properties come in handy. Try to build a friendship with someone at the Appraisal District. After a while, you may be able to have them look up a property for you if you can't drive down there.

The owner of the property may not be a person. It may look like this: LTK Investments, L.P. That's O.K. The important part is to get the correct mailing address.

Once you have the correct mailing address and name, it's time to move to the next step.

Contacting the owner

Your first contact should always be in the form of a letter. At the back of this book, I have enclosed my standard letter, but you may want to change it to one of your own creation.

It's important that your letter be totally professional looking. Be sure it is typed with no typos. This is where your good looking letterhead is essential. Attach your good looking business card on the top left with a paper clip.

Once you have sent the letter, to the exact name and address that you found on the property tax records, you have to sit back and wait and see if you get a call. Sometimes you get a call immediately, other times it takes weeks, and sometimes it never comes at all. If the call never comes at all, here are some additional follow-up steps to take:

- Write additional letters. Never send more than one per week. Keep them short and upbeat. Never sound threatening or mad or they won't call you.

- Drop by the mailing address, and see if they will talk to you in person. I've stopped by every form of office; from brake shop to attorney. In those cases, always wear a conservative suit and tie as it will greatly improve the odds of them meeting with you. Always be cordial and go in with the mindset that you want to give them money. Never start off with "you wouldn't call me so I had to come by..."

- Drop by neighboring landowners. Never tell them you are with a billboard company – they will not help you in any way. Imply that you are a real estate guy interested in the property. See if they have the owners name and phone number, or would pass on your business card to the owner when they see them.

I once had the name and address of a property owner that I wanted to build a billboard on. He would never call me. So I started to drop by his house once a week. It was a huge estate, and a maid in uniform would greet me at the door, and take my business card. After months of this, the guy calls me and says, "What do I have to do to get you to stop coming by my house?" I said, "Sign my billboard lease." He said, "O.K., I'll sign your lease if you promise never to contact me again." He did, and I did.

Meeting with the owner

If you need to meet with the owner of the land prior to getting them to sign a lease, here are a few tips to give you the best shot at making a deal:

- Already have the ground lease typed up when you go to the meeting. If the opportunity comes up, have them sign the lease before they can change their mind.

- Keep instilling the idea that you are only leasing nine square feet of ground space (roughly the amount used by a single pole steel structure). This will help make the amount you are paying "per square foot" really impressive.

- Put your magnetic sign on the door of your vehicle before you arrive – the owner will be sizing you up by the vehicle you are driving, and all owners love big companies. Big companies make them feel secure.

- Go in with the mental attitude that you are a consultant working for the owner, trying to help him get extra income from his property. Never argue with the owner, or act in any manner other than completely respectful – after telling you "no" the owner may change his mind, but if he doesn't like you, he will never call you again.

- If you can, wear a tie (the coat is not essential). This helps reinforce the "big company" image that owners love.

If you leave the lease with the owner, try to get him to commit to a timetable of when you should contact him again. When you call on this date, start out with "I was just calling to touch base and see if you have had a chance to read that contract." It may require several of these calls, and missed deadlines, before he decides.

Signing the lease

The first thing we all have to agree on is that there is no exactly right or wrong lease. There are basic components to any billboard lease, but the terms may differ somewhat based on how good a location it is, how good a negotiator the landowner is, and how bad you want it and are willing to take risk.

A billboard lease should contain the following:

- A start date
- A reasonable term (my standard was 15 years with a 15 year option. I've seen leases as short as 5 years.)
- A percent of advertising revenue to landowner (industry norm is 15% to 20%), a fixed monthly or annual amount to landowner regardless of whether or not the sign is rented, or both.
- A provision for removal of the sign (ranging from never to the event of construction requiring removal).

- A provision whereby the owner cannot allow anything to obstruct the billboard (planting a tree, erecting a flag, etc.)

- A timetable on what happens with the rent between when the lease is signed and the sign is built (we always tried to have the rent start once the sign was built, but often the owner wanted a firm start date).

- An escape clause for you if you can't rent the sign or can't get a permit.

- Some nominal amount of money to change hands (check the laws of your state) so that the lease is binding.

- A provision that the landowner has the right to sign the lease (example; you sign up the lease with John and it turns out Larry is the real owner and your lease is worthless. This happens frequently.)

I have included a copy of my old standard lease, but you definitely need your <u>own</u> legal counsel to construct the lease. My lease is old and may not be valid in your state.

Getting the permits

In most places you will need two permits: 1) State 2) City. To apply for these permits you will probably need the following items:

- A copy of your signed lease (be sure to white out the dollar amounts, because it will become public record and your competitors can read it).

- A letter from the owner (normally a form that authorizes you to pull the permit).

- A fairly detailed diagram as to where the sign will go, including measurements to the foot of setback and distance from property lines and other nearby billboards.

- Engineered, sealed drawings of the billboard you are building, showing the approved windload.

- Application fee.

Be sure to be as charming as possible with these people, because you will probably be stuck with them for your entire career. There is very little turnover in the public sector. If you make a bad impression, they can really make your life difficult.

Normally, the state permit must be obtained before the city.

This information is all general. You must get with the process in the market you are working in. It varies all over the map.

You can get the engineered drawings from the steel fabricator who builds billboards in the market you are in.

Now What Do I Do? <u>I can't find one billboard lease and i've looked everywhere.</u>

This may be hard to accept, but if any idiot could find plentiful billboard leases, then there would be no point in doing it. There is no reason for embarrassment if you can't find any initially. It took me two years to find my first five. Some markets are <u>completely</u> exhausted. But take heart, here's a list of tricks to get your search jumpstarted.

- **Go one more sign out.** Find a road that is a little out of town. A place where the billboards end due to a lack of enthusiasm. But an area that you believe will grow over time. Find the landowner down the street from the last built billboard and lease it. Sometimes, if you're lucky, this site is only there because the other billboard companies always figured it would be there if they needed it and its fundamentals are already better than you thought.

- **Build ahead of the highway.** Most municipalities have very specific timetables for the construction and expansion of their roads and highways. You can sometimes tie up some great locations on highways that have not even been built yet. You can sign up the lease before the exact right-of-way has even been acquired. Be sure that the lease payment does not begin until the sign is built.

- **Re-zone the land.** If you find a piece of land that is legal for a billboard in every respect except the zoning, try rezoning it. This is very complicated, because it can cause significant tax problems for the landowner in some instances. But often, the owner was going to do it anyway, to increase the land's value and won't care.

- **Obtain a variance.** Some cities, especially small towns, would be open to giving you the variance to build a sign when their ordinance prohibits them, if you give them something in return that they want. I successfully did this four times, each time trading the city the free use of one side of the billboard for finite period of time (normally two years).

- **Create a commercial district.** Some billboard ordinances define a commercial zoning district based on use rather than zoning. Many require two businesses side-by-side to qualify for the zoning needed for a billboard. If this is the case, look into the possibility of "creating" a business next to an existing business to make this possible. You will be amazed at how easy it is to be made a qualifying business. Sometimes a cheap rentable building and three old junk cars makes you a respectable "used car" business. Once the billboard is built, sometimes the business can close without affecting your permit. This whole concept is very tricky – get legal advice before you start.

- **Make the junk location into a winner.** If there is a legal location that you passed on because of tree obstructions, think again. You may be able to go to the owners of the trees and obtain a "vegetation easement" to remove or trim back the offending trees. There was once a very valuable location in Dallas, TX that was successfully, and cleverly, made into a winner in this manner. Sometimes, the neighbor will let you do this for free.

- **Build a "weather station" billboard.** This was one of my most successful concepts. Go way out of town where billboards are legal, but almost nobody builds them due to poor demand by advertisers. Build an inexpensive sign. Try to rent it, but make sure your phone number is always visible on it, even if it is just on the skirt under the ad. Wait for something big to happen. An example was the small sign I built in Terrell, Texas. Everybody thought it was a loser, because the market was so small. Then I received a call from the marketing department of a huge outlet mall that was secretly about to be built next door. I ran out and tied up every billboard location on both sides of the highway for several miles. I had those signs up and finished before anyone knew what was happening. When the news came out, I had a virtual monopoly, and all the other billboard companies were left out in the cold.

- **Replace an obsolete billboard.** Those old wooden billboards, half falling down, or taking up valuable permits. Go to the landowner and, if the lease is expiring or expired, offer to replace it with your sign and pay them more money. Be careful not to commit "tortuous interference". This legal term refers to the illegal act of convincing the landowner to terminate a non-terminable contract. Remember the Pennzoil scandal of the 80's? Talk to your attorney about this one before you do it.

Remember that Wal-Mart began in small towns and, once a hit, moved into the big cities. You may have more luck finding billboard locations in more rural areas initially, and that is a perfectly normal state of affairs.

I've found some legal locations, but my owners won't sign a lease

Here are some creative ideas for the "hard to sign" owner:

- Offer a signing bonus. Add this expense into your billboard loan. Make it meaningful. $1,000 cash. A new stainless Rolex. A lot will depend on the location. It works for sports stars.

- Offer to prepay several years upfront. I have seen companies pay up to ten years in advance. Make sure that you pay nothing until the sign is built. This is a very risky thing to do; you have added a lot of debt to the sign.

- Offer the owner one side of the sign for a specified time for free as an inducement. Maybe his ego is large and he wants

to put himself on the sign for a while (very attractive sometimes to ranchers with champion horses or livestock).

- Make the owner a partner in the sign. Make him a 50% or
  less partner, receiving 50% of the net. See if you can make
  him put up 50% of the money. Sometimes, you can get
  him to sign if you let him own the sign and you receive a
  percentage of the net for managing it and leasing it.

- Buy the land from the owner, trim off the billboard site
  and re-sell the land. We called this "buy/trim/flip". It is extremely risky. You could be caught with some unsold land
  that the billboard will never support the payments on.

As you can see, there are options, but none is as good as the old-
fashioned lease.

The other alternative: Buying existing billboards

About 30% of my billboards were acquired by me from other billboard companies. These acquisitions were in several types of transactions:

- **Buying obsolete signs.** One of my most unusual transactions was the purchase of all of the Stuckey's signs in east Texas. Stuckey's is an old franchise, most of which went out of business decades ago. The home office for these signs was in Atlanta, Georgia. To my amazement, no one had ever contacted them about buying their old, dilapidated wooden signs. They didn't realize that each old, nasty sign came with a special prize, a priceless billboard permit. I fixed each of them up to like-new and it was very profitable (about a 100% return on equity, annually).

  This maneuver whetted my appetite for more, and shortly thereafter I bought some of the abandoned Terry's franchise signs, and did it again.

- **Buying "dog" signs.** Often, the "big" billboard companies have signs that, for whatever reason, they find unprofitable. These signs may have blemishes that you can quickly and inexpensively fix. For example, I bought a steel billboard that had poor visibility due to tree obstructions. As discussed earlier, I went to the neighbors and bought, for almost nothing, the right to trim the trees. Bingo, great sign once again. Another example was the sign I bought in downtown Dallas that the "big" guys couldn't rent because there was a "Park Here" sign right in front of the advertising space. Again, I went to the parking company and they agreed to lower their sign out of the way if I'd pay for it. Another strange example was the sign in the impoverished part of town that had not been rented for years. I rented it almost immediately to bail bondsmen and injury attorneys.

- ***Buying Signs Out of Bankruptcy or Financial Trouble.*** Several of my smartest maneuvers during the 1989-92 recession were the purchase of distressed billboards. Normally, I had to wait through extensive bankruptcy proceedings. I remember spending days as an observer of mediations. Enduring crying billboard owners or co-signers. But in the end, it was all worth it. I paid what these people thought, at that time, was way too much money. But I had faith that things would turn around.

- ***Signs I paid retail for.*** Occasionally, I would find a sign for sale that I thought had a great and endless future, due to the general growth of the market it was in. Buying such a sign requires a true belief in the market, as you are putting a premium of debt on the sign, and in any market there are ups and downs in the economic cycle. I've seen rents fluctuate from $3,000 per month to $300 per month at the drop of a hat. You have to have the confidence during the down cycles that it will come back.

Considerations When Buying a Billboard

Buying a billboard is no different from building a billboard except for:

- You don't have to take the risk and time of building it
- You pay a premium for not doing the above

Buying a billboard is more about economics because your only focus is in the numbers, not the uncertainties you face when building it such as visibility, etc. Everything is completely up and tangible.

There are, however, four important risks you must be certain of:

- *Illegal signs.* Make sure the billboard sign you are buying has all of the necessary state and city permits

- *Not overhanging the neighbor.* Make sure the sign is completely on the correct property. Not one inch of the sign can cross-over. And check the setback requirements.

- *Make sure the electricity to the sign is connected.* You would be surprised at how often someone builds a billboard without considering how to get power to it. Sometimes it is very expensive to run power to the sign and sometimes it is impossible.

- *Make sure the lease is in effect.* Demand to talk to the landowner. Make certain that he is o.k. with the sign and acknowledges receipt of the ground rent.

It is customary, when buying a billboard to obtain an inspection period, normally 30 days, and a financing contingency period of 30 to 60 days. Don't do any work until this is in writing and signed by the seller. Otherwise you are wasting your time.

The Real Economics of Billboard Ownership

You've either got a billboard lease and permit at this point, or an existing billboard under contract. How do you decide whether to build it or buy it?

Let's look at each part of the Income Statement for a billboard.

Income

Rent: This is going to be the gross rent paid to you per month by the advertiser on the sign. If you have two sides of the sign, then you will have two rents coming in. Be sure to be reasonable in your expectations, don't use the highest rent average on the street. Take 20% off or so, to account for lesser times, or more if you can. Also factor in some vacancy. Vacancy would be at least two months or so between advertisers.

Expenses

Agency: Most advertising agencies receive a percentage of the gross rent, normally 16.6%. If you rent your billboard without using an advertising agency, then this number is -0-.

Paint: Or more likely 'vinyl' today, this cost is the cost of production of the advertisement. Your ad lease may require that you repaint the sign every 6 months. Or it may be a year between paint jobs. Be sure to factor in the other costs that will come up, such as scraping down or replacing the panels periodically, and replacing the vinyl if you do not paint it.

Electricity: If your billboard is lighted at night (which almost all the good ones are), you will have an electricity cost. If you call the power company in your area with the total wattage you will be burning, and the number of hours per day, then they can give you a pretty accurate estimate to use.

Management Fee: It costs you something to drive out and look at the sign, to sell the advertising and keep your phone line going. At first, this number is onerous, but as you add signs and split the cost, it becomes more manageable. The target is 5%.

Repair and Maintenance: Like any other structure, your billboard will need continual upkeep to remain safe and in operation. These items will include replacement of light bulbs, replacement of panels, replacement of safety equipment, repainting the structure, replacing the time clock, and perhaps an annual or less frequent inspection of the structure for structural safety issues (rust, bad welds, loose bolts, etc.)

Insurance: You will need at minimum liability insurance to operate a billboard, and possibly some form of physical damage insurance in the event of a catastrophic loss (similar to car insurance options). Contact an insurance agent for these rates and options.

Property Tax: You may (based on the municipality) be taxed for the billboard's value as personal property tax. Consult your taxing authority.

Licenses and Permits: Some cities make you pay an annual fee for a billboard, some states do as well.

Other: Some other costs include landscaping (sometimes you have to mow around the billboard or at least weed-eat), replacing private power drops, just anything that may pop up.

EBITDA: The difference between your rent income and these costs is your EBITDA, which stands for earnings before interest, taxes, depreciation and amortization. This is the money that will go to make your loan payment. If this number is negative, you have to really give this a second thought. While owning a billboard sounds impressive at a cocktail party, the whole point is to make money, and if you build a billboard that is guaranteed to lose money, it may not be much fun for you. And then there is a problem that you can't really sell it, because nobody wants a guaranteed loser billboard.

If this number is positive, see how much debt it will support. This magic number should be your guideline for how much you have to spend to either build it or buy it.

But let's first look at the kind of loans you can get, to see what your budget is.

Getting a Loan for a Billboard

This is an area that I feel I have a lot of expertise in, since my mastery of it was the reason I could buy so aggressively during the 1980's savings and loan crisis.

In the world of billboard lending you will have basically four avenues:

- *Your local small bank.* This would be your "hometown" bank, where you probably do your checking at. These banks rely a lot on your "character", and don't put a lot of faith in a billboard as collateral. Everyone should start here. Even if the bank turns you down, which it probably will, you can start the timeclock on building a relationship, because if you keep on brown-nosing this guy, eventually you can probably get a loan as a test. Even if you can get your first loan here, they will probably freak out by your tenth sign or so, or you'll hit their loan limit for a single customer. Hit as many local banks as you can – hit every one in your town. I used to start off by hitting 100 or so. You never know when you might get lucky.

- *The national bank.* Such as Bank of America. These banks allow you to escape the "loan limit" problem of the local bank, as they have enormous deposits and enormous loan limits. However, they are very tough on underwriting standards. You'll need near perfect credit and some solid cash down, and very good B.S. with the loan officer. They will understand the collateral more than the local bank, but there are still other options to explore. Again, hit every single one you can. If nothing else, the practice will make you a better talker.

- ***The lease/purchase lender.*** This is where I hit my home run. It was a lender named "Courtesy Leasing" out of Montgomery, Alabama. They are still around, and I heartily recommend them. At this type of lender, you don't have to educate them on the collateral. Plus, their analysis of your loan is helpful because they have good ideas and real-life experience to draw from. The best part is that they are not normally subject to the extreme withdrawal from lending that the regular banks are during recessions. Since they only make loans on a finite type of collateral, they could care less if single-family home loans collapse, or the stock market collapses because that has no affect on their loan pool. When I changed over from local bank and national bank lending to lease/purchase lending, my life improved 1000%. Of course, lease/purchase borrowing is a little unusual and a little more expensive. The lender effectively owns the billboard, and you lease it for a set amount each month and then buy it at the end for the residual value (just like a car lease). I don't have one bad thing to say about this type of program.

  Courtesy Outdoor Finance

  P.O. Box 4308

  Montgomery, AL 36103

  1-800-253-6504

  www.courtesyoutdoorfinance.com

- ***The wealthy individual lender.*** Under this option, you borrow money from someone who has capital, or this person obtains the loans for you. This option is chock full of pitfalls. First, there is no regulatory body presiding over the wealthy individual, unlike the bank, to govern their behavior with you. They may become very erratic, or renegotiate the terms with you frequently. Secondly, the wealthy individual will want equity in your billboards, as well as interest. He will want to get repaid in full, plus interest, plus a carried interest of up to 50%. People normally take this option first, but I can tell you from experience, this should be your last option, only used when all other options fail. I have known many a hard-working entrepreneur who has been wiped out through a soured relationship with the wealthy individual investor.

Deciding What Kind of Billboard to Build

There are a number of different billboard options to meet almost any budget. It is very important that you match the correct billboard type to the correct location. Otherwise, you are liable to overbuild or underbuild your location, which will penalize you greatly down the road.

Billboards come in three standardized formats. These are the painted bulletin (14' x 48') or (10'6" x 36'), the 30 sheet poster (12' x 24') and the 8 sheet (about 6' x 12'). If you want to sell your billboard to a big company down the road for a lot of money, it will have to be one of these three sizes, or they won't buy them. Why? Big companies are fully standardized and sell to national advertisers who have their ads ready in these three sizes. Customize to fit your billboard? Not a chance. If you had the best billboard location in the world and it was not one of these standard sizes, they absolutely would not buy it from you. So the first question before building or buying your billboard is: is this location worthy of selling to a big company down the road? If the answer is yes, then you must go with one of these three sizes. If however, you are in a rural location that no big company would ever want, or are buying an old billboard that already is of a different size, then and only then can you build whatever is visible or suits your fancy. However, my bet is that you should build with an eye to selling out down the road to a big company.

If you decide to build one of these three sizes, then the key question is what will hold it up? There are four possible formats:

- **Single steel pole.** Also called a monopole. This is the Cadillac of the industry, and where all the big money is when you sell out down the road. This is also the most expensive way to build a billboard.

- *Steel multi-pole.* This is sometimes a less expensive alternative to the unipole. It all really depends on the cost of steel and if there's some cheap pipe at the steel fabricator's shop. For resale value, the monopole is worth more, so to go to the steel multi-pole, it would have to be a big discount.

- *Steel I-beam.* This is a very standard design for the 12' x 24' 30-sheet poster sign. The kits are very affordable, and I do not believe that I-beams would hurt your re-sale value, but rather provide a huge benefit to low cost.

- *Wooden multi-pole.* This is the billboard construction that looks like telephone poles. That's because they are telephone poles. Although the cheapest way to build a billboard, these things look bad, have poor re-sale value and fall down. We had at least three catastrophic failures of these structures and in high winds they are prone to snap at the ground and fall down. We were lucky – there was nothing underneath them in their rural setting. Had there been a structure or a person, it would have been a huge liability nightmare.

- *Digital Billboards and Trivisions:* These are the new technologies to maximize the potential revenue for certain billboard locations. Trivisions are those signs you've seen that "change" every 10 seconds or so to 1 of 3 different ads. The billboard face is made up of hundreds of 4" wide triangles that move on a chain. This allows you to have three ads instead of one.

A digital billboard is a sign in which the entire sign changes with an infinite variety of ads (like a TV screen). They range in how elaborate they are from the "time and temperature" style to the full "movie screen" type.

To warrant this type of project (and these can be very expensive… up to 6 digits), you must have a landmark location – either one with unbelievable traffic (250,000+ cars/day) or an unbelievable setting (right in front of the Grauman's Chinese Theater in Hollywood). It is unlikely that your billboard will be worthy of this initially. However, these technologies might make an expensive billboard you are buying make financial sense.

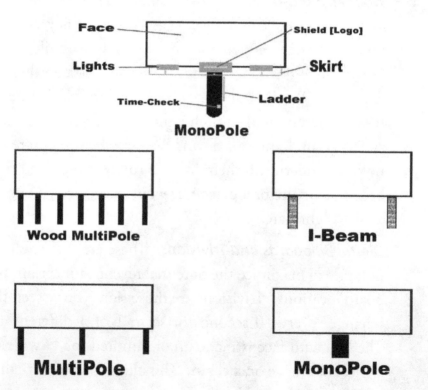

In summary, it is in your best interest to stick to the sizes and configurations of the big companies, since they will demand this similarity if you try to sell to them down the road. Stick to steel construction on anything but a remote rural billboard, but look for the price anomalies brought about by some cheap steel at the fabricator's yard.

Osha and other Complications

When building the billboard, be <u>sure</u> to comply with OSHA (Occupational Safety and Hazards Administration) requirements. It adds some significant expense to the structure (safety chords, additional ladders, etc.) but it is essential for two reasons:

- *It's the Law.* If someone gets hurt on the sign and it's because you violated OSHA, you are in big trouble. Maybe even jail time. And they also do spot inspections to see if you are in compliance. If they catch you, the fines are enormous.

- *When you go to sell out down the road,* the big companies are going to require that you have it. If you don't, you'll have to retrofit it, and that costs more than doing it originally.

Some fabricators will tell you its overkill. Let OSHA decide that. Stay within the law and you'll be very glad you did later.

Selling Your Billboard Lease to a Competitor

O.K. on this sign you've decided to sell your lease rather than build it. That may be a good decision. There's no right or wrong answer, and this will depend entirely on you and your circumstances.

- *First thing you do* is making sure you have all of the required permits and that you are 100% in line with your lease. Because if you don't the unhappy bidder may try to screw you over by stealing your location or landowner. Also, during the examination of your lease and permit by the winning bidder, errors can show up and blow the whole deal.

- *If you are sure everything is correct,* then you should make a list of every billboard company in the market. Even those who aren't in the yellow pages because they only have one or two signs (you've seen their name on the shield of their billboard). These are your "A" list of buyers. Put an ad in the paper under "real estate for sale". I know it is not real estate, but that's where the buyers are, and it's sort of an income property. Anyone who responds to this, or any other advertisement, becomes your "B" list.

- *Put together a package* including all of the reasons why this is a billboard location someone would want to buy. Attach a map showing the location, and some photos showing what the sign would look like (a white or black billboard-shaped box on the photo as a mock-up). Price it at about 30% more than you really want, since nobody will offer you your asking price.

Get this package to everyone on list "A" and list "B" as fast as possible. Don't hold back, and don't stagger sending it because you are afraid you will be drowning in calls. Because in reality, only a small portion will have any interest anyway. Once you have an interested party, this becomes your "Hot Prospect" list.

- *After that, it's all about* working your Hot Prospect list. Keep in constant contact with each one until he gives you his offer. Play the best offers off against each other and you will end up with one person who is clearly your best shot. Try to get the deal done as soon as possible. Remember the quote "Time Kills Deals". That means time is not your ally. It is not common to use title companies or attorneys to sell a lease. All you need is a valid assignment of lease and permit document, including any necessary permit assignment applications to the state and city, and the buyers check.

- *What if nobody will make a bid?* It probably means your location is too weak. That's a good indication that you probably should not build it. But it may be worthwhile to go back to the landowner and tell them you've decided the lease is too weak right now, but would like to pay him maybe $100 a year to hold it until the economy strengthens. A year from now, it may be worth something.

Selling Your Billboard that You've Built to a Competitor

So you built your billboard and now you want to sell it. Follow the same directions as in the above paragraph. Only this time you can have real photos to show of the actual signs, and you will need to include the advertising lease and rates. It is my experience that a built billboard is 10 times easier to sell than a lease, because the buyer can tangibly see what he's buying. The only problem is now rather than 100% profit on the sale, you have to subtract what you spent to build it to get your true profit number.

What if Nobody Wants to Buy Your Built Billboard?

There is a trick to selling a built billboard that nobody wants. I've done it before and it works every time. Here's how you do it:

- Write down the name of every advertiser on every sign in the vicinity of your billboard.

- Get the mailing address of each advertiser.

- Write a letter to each one offering your billboard space at a ridiculous price (if the going rate is $500 per month offer it $200 as an introductory price).

- Sit back and wait.

What will happen is that news of the $200 rent will get back to the other owners, and the one with the most to lose will call you and buy your sign just to get such an idiot loose canon out of the marketplace. Of course, the downside is you will have to honor the $200 introductory price. Try to tie it to a three year lease at the standard $500 per month, so that your average rent is not too bad.

Selling Advertising Space

In my heyday, I used to rent 15 billboard faces per month. That's one every two calendar days. How did I do it?

- *Make a list* of every advertiser on a competitors sign in the vicinity of your sign. This is your "Move-Over" list.

- *Buy the labels* for every business in the zip code of your billboard from a direct mail company. Sort out the ones that are completely unlikely to advertise such as dry cleaners and such. Do a direct mail piece to all of these people; an 8 ½" x 11" sheet printed on two sides, with every possible benefit of advertising on your sign(A sample is at the back of this book). When businesses call you, make this your "Top Prospect" list.

- *Put your phone number* very visibly on the blank advertising panels on your sign.

These four efforts should yield something. If nothing happens, start phoning your lists. My pitch was "You would take my sign for $1, so I know you want it. How low would I have to go to rent it to you?"

In the end, you will rent it to the highest bidder. Be sure to include the cost of production of the ad and lease length in your final decision on the best bid. If you have to paint the sign every six months on a one year lease, you will be better off with a once a year paint on a three year lease.

Subleasing the Sign to a Big Rival

Sometimes the best thing to do with your advertising space is to sublease it to a big sign company with rotary accounts. They will not pay you as much as you had figured on for a regular customer, but the trade off is that you have no production cost or vacancy downtime. Plus, you can sometimes use the sublease as collateral at a small town bank.

I was at one time one of the largest sub-lessors to Foster & Kleiser in Dallas (the biggest billboard company at that time). Their payments barely covered my note payment, but the solidity let me sleep at night. And when the economy fell apart in 1989-1992, it sure felt good to have signs 100% leased.

Don't be shy about calling the big guys and seeing if they're interested. Developing a dialogue with them may be beneficial down the road, like buying their "dog" signs.

Servicing the Customer

Once you have rented the billboard and installed the ad, the client only wants three things from you:

- *Make sure that the advertisement is* not damaged in any way from high winds or temperature changes, or bird droppings. If you see a problem, fix it immediately. Don't wait for the client to call you. It will cost you the same to fix it, but the client won't trust you anymore.

- *Make sure the lights work* (if it is a lighted billboard). Be sure to re-adjust the on switch when it gets dark earlier. If a bulb goes out, get it fixed ASAP. I know it's a big pain to drive your signs at night, but when your client proudly tells his wife, "Here comes my billboard", only to find it illegible in the dark, you have lost a client for life. Use an electric "eye" that automatically turns on at dark, if possible.

- *Accurate billing.* Make sure your bills go out timely and with the correct amount on them. And if the client over-pays, send them a refund immediately.

You will soon find that the billboard business is really pretty low stress to manage, and billboards are pretty low maintenance. But when problems do pop up, treat them like you would want to be treated.

The Most Important Efficiency of Numbers: Rotary

There is a power in having multiple billboards that is far more important than better deals on volume light bulbs. All the big companies know it but don't discuss it much. It's the concept of the "rotary" billboard. In this program, a billboard is changed or "rotated" among a group of signs, so that the advertiser gets not just one location, but several. The beauty to it is that you can sell the advertiser on the one great location and he's O.K. with the several dreadful ones. It allows you to have a product that only the big companies have to offer, and it allows you to unload bad locations at good prices. The advertiser seldom seems to keep tabs on where the ad is at. If you ever get big enough to have a rotary program, go for it. It's the most important "volume" advantage you can get.

Looking to the Future

The billboard business in the U.S. is over 100 years old. There is not a lot of new product development out there to be worried about. The biggest change I've seen was the invention of painting the ad on vinyl, brought about in the 1980's. The sizes of signs have been static for decades, as have the tools of the trade (leases, rates, etc.).

It is refreshing to have an industry so old and worn in, with no new technologies to knock you out overnight.

The bad part is that a lot of the locations have been exhausted. Yet new locations come into being constantly, every time a new road is built or expanded. Or every time a city grows and takes in more land or more businesses.

If you apply yourself, things will come your way. It takes a while to understand how to do it, just like anything else.

However, this is a worthwhile investment of your time, because the profits can be astounding. Here's a few real examples:

- A billboard on a major highway in a decent market can sell for $100,000 to $300,000+. The profit on that one sign, after construction cost, can buy you a house.

- An old wooden sign that I bought in 1982 for $4,000 generated $21,000 a year of income to me for 14 straight years until I sold it, for an additional profit of $60,000. That's $354,000 profit on a $4,000 investment. Again, can buy you a house.

- A decent lease on a lesser road can bring you $15,000 cash profit. Four leases like that can buy you a house, or at least the down payment.

Good luck and good hunting!

Definitions and Terminology

"Billboard" is a common word for poster panels and bulletins. There are three standard kinds of billboards:

Bulletins

Standard sizes:

> *14 by 48 feet (672 sq. ft.), plus extensions*
> *10'6" by 36 feet (378 sq. ft.), plus extensions*

Bulletins are used to display painted or computer-generated vinyl images and are found in high density traffic areas, such as highways and Interstates. Bulletins are most often leased for multi-month contract periods, most often 12 or more months.

However, a rotary bulletin is actually a group of bulletins on which an advertiser's message is displayed on one bulletin for short intervals, usually 60 days, and then repeatedly moved to another bulletin in another area of the market. This rotation helps achieve broader market coverage.

30-Sheet Poster Panels

Standard size: 12 by 25 feet (300 sq. ft.)

Thirty-sheet poster panels are widely distributed throughout markets on primary and secondary roadways. Different levels of market coverage are achieved through 25, 50, 75, and 100 GRP showings. The computer-generated vinyl, lithographed, or screen-printed posters are usually displayed for 30 days.

8-Sheet Poster Panels (Junior Posters)

Standard size: 6 by 12 feet (72 sq. ft.)

- Eight-sheet poster panels are generally contracted for 30 day periods to reach pedestrian and vehicular traffic. They are frequently used in high density urban neighborhoods and suburban shopping areas as well as point-of-purchase locales. Different levels of market coverage are achieved through 25, 50, 75, and 100 GRP showings.

Out of Home Media

Out of home (OOH) media broadly describes a variety of advertising vehicles which reach consumers where they shop and travel. OOH media include:

Transit/Airport/Malls

Busses (sides and fully-wrapped), trains, station platforms, commuter rail cards, underground, airports, malls, trucks, taxi tops.

Street Furniture

Bus shelters, phone kiosks, newsstands, circular and interactive kiosks.

Spectaculars and Walls

Large displays draped or hung on sides of buildings, murals, animatronics displays.

Abandoned Billboard - Billboard in which the current owner has given up on and is no longer being actively maintained or leased.

Allotment - The number of units required to achieve a desired GRP (showing) in a certain market.

Ambient Media - Non traditional outdoor advertising medium and includes such media as mobile billboards, atm advertising, street and other venue advertising.

Approach - The distance from where the billboard can first be seen to the point where it is passed by.

Apron - The horizontal panel below the face of the billboard. Here you will often find the sign companies name

Audited Circulation - This is the traffic count certified by TAB (Traffic Audit Bureau), an independent auditing company that verifies traffic counts.

Availability or Avails - The billboards in your inventory that are available at any given time.

Back-to-Back - A sign with 2 faces that are back to back to each other (ie: one side can be seen going north and the other going south.

Billboard (Board) - Large format outdoor advertising displays that are meant to be viewed from extended distances.

Bleed Poster - Where the poster is designed to make the copy fill the entire space inside the billboards frame or trim.

Bleed Through - Where the previous ad copy can be seen through the current ad copy

Catwalk - A platform that is used as a walkway in order to access and change the billboard face.

Circulation - The amount of traffic in a given market and includes vehicle and pedestrian traffic.

Conforming Sign - A billboard that is placed on a legal site and is in compliance with current government requirements.

Copy - The actual message or artwork displayed on the billboard

CPM (Cost Per Thousand) - The common method for comparing advertising costs. The CPM is the media cost for generating one thousand views. It is calculated by dividing the monthly cost by the monthly circulation in thousands.

Cross Read (Left Hand View) - This occurs when the occupants in a vehicle have to look across oncoming traffic to read a billboard's message

Coverage - Refers to the percentage of a given market that is exposed to an advertising location.

Daily Effective Circulation (DEC) - The number of people that are aged 18 and over and have the opportunity to see the message on the billboard during an average day.

Display Period - The amount of time an individual billboard campaign is viewed.

Direct Read (Right Hand View) - This is when occupants in a vehicle are able to read a billboard without looking across oncoming traffic.

Distraction - Anything that competes for the billboards viewers – such as other billboards, trees, traffic signs, etc.

Double Face Signs - Signs with 2 faces that can be seen from the same direction.

Dominant Estate – Refers to the interest in a land parcel that benefits from an easement encumbering a piece of adjoining land.

Easement Appurtenant - An easement benefiting an interest in an adjoining property. The benefiting property interest is called a dominant estate, and the encumbered or burdened property interest is called a servient estate.

Easement in Gross - An easement that benefits a legal person rather than an interest in an adjoining property. With an easement in gross, there is no dominant estate. The encumbered or burdened property interest is called a servient estate.

Embellishment (aka Cut-outs) - Special effects or additions to a billboard that enhance or extend beyond the standard face of the billboard to attract more attention.

Exposure - The instance of seeing an advertising message.

Exposure Time - The amount of time the advertising message is in view to the intended viewer.

Face - The area of the billboard that contains the advertising message – one billboard structure may have more than one face.

Facing - The direction that the billboard faces. For example, a north facing billboard sign face would be visible to southbound traffic.

Flagging - When the paper or vinyl on a billboard is loose and ripples in the wind.

Footings – This refers to the base of the billboard sign that supports the poles or other supports.

Frequency - The number of times a person is exposed to a certain billboard ad message in a certain time period.

GRP (Gross Rating Points) - Refers to the total number of impressions delivered by a billboard or ad message and is expressed as a percentage of the markets population. This is measured on a daily basis and is often referred to a showing. If the sign has a rating of 40 GRP's, this would indicate that approximately 40% of the population in that market will see the sign each day.

Illegal Sign - A billboard unlawfully erected or maintained. The sign may be illegal or the site may be illegal, or both.

Just Compensation - This is the amount paid for the rights and interests of the billboard sign owner and landowner and that is required by the Highway Beautification Acts and amendments.

Lease - This is the agreement by which the possession or use of the land or other interests is granted to another person or entity for a specified purpose.

Lessee – Refers to the leaseholder, the one who owns the billboard and pays the landowner.

Lessor – Refers to the Land owner – the one whom the lessee will pay the rent to.

Line of Sight - When viewing one billboard, all the other billboards that can be viewed at that location are in the line of sight of that billboard.

List of Locations - All the locations that are in a certain outdoor advertising campaign.

Mall Displays - Advertising displays located in high traffic areas of shopping centers.

Market - An area that can be divided either economically, geographically, politically, etc.

Mass Transit Advertising - Advertising on public vehicles such as buses, trains, subways, etc.

Message Area - The area of the billboard that is available to display the advertising copy.

Mobile Billboard - A vehicle or trailer that has one or more poster panel units. The vehicle can either be stationary or driven around the target areas.

Multifaced Signs – Billboards with more than one face (doubles, stacked, back-to-backs, V signs, triples, etc)

Nonconforming Sign - A billboard that may have been legal when it was erected but now does not comply with new laws and regulations – AKA "Gandfathered Signs"

> *In some cases the sign location is conforming but the sign is not. In these cases the sign may be replaced at some future time by bringing it up to code.*

OAAA (Outdoor Advertising Association of America) - The national trade association that represents the out-of-home media companies and the industry as a whole.

Off Premise Sign - A billboard that is promoting a specific business, product, service, or event that is not sold, built, or carried out at the property where the billboard is located.

On Premise Sign - A billboard that is promoting a specific business, product, service, or event and is sold, built, or carried out at the property where the sign is located.

Out-of-Home Media - Includes all forms of outdoor advertising placed to be viewed by consumers.

Painted Bulletin - Billboards in which the message is painted directly on the vinyl or structure itself.

Plant - Refers to an outdoor advertising company and all of its locations in a given market.

Permanent Bulletins - Are typically 14' by 48' and contain the same message for long periods (usually at least one year). These are used to build strong brand recognition in good markets.

Permit - A license granted by the city, state, or county to authorize a billboard structure at a specific location.

Poster - The term for the messages posted on a billboard.

Poster Panel - A billboard that accommodates either an 8-Sheet or 30-Sheet display.

Premier Panel – Refers to a 30-sheet poster sign that is covered in vinyl across the entire face.

Production - Refers to the process of digitally creating artwork onto the vinyl display surface.

Reach - The percentage of the targeting population that will be potentially exposed to the advertising message during a specific period of time.

Riding the Showing - Refers to the physical inspection of all the billboards in the advertising program. Basically a drive by to see where your ads are located.

Rotary Program - A program in which the bulletin is moved to different locations in the same market to increase and balance the reach in that market.

Setback - The distance the billboard is from the traffic area. The greater the setback, the farther the sign is from the traffic.

Servient Estate – An interest in land that is encumbered by an easement.

Showing - The total number of units in the advertising program, or more specifically, the total number of GRP's delivered by a given number of panels.

Sign Face - The area of the billboard that contains the advertising message – one structure may have more than one face.

Sign Facing - The direction that the billboard faces.

Snipe - An adhesive strip added to the message to change or modify the message – often used to announce special events, price changes, or dates.

Spectaculars - These are often large and expensive and custom built for the advertiser. They have no standard dimensions and often incorporate digital or other motions. You will often see these signs in major downtown areas and high traffic locations.

Stacked Panels - Two advertising panels that are part of one structure and are built on top of each other and face the same direction.

Street Furniture - Refers to advertising displays nearby foot traffic and usually provides a public service such as bus transit shelters, kiosks, benches, etc.

TAB (Traffic Audit Bureau) - The independent auditing bureau responsible for verifying traffic counts and circulations in a given market. The bureau is a non-profit organization that is supported by advertisers, agencies, and plant operators.

Target Audience - The actual consumer group that the advertising message is directed to.

Taxi Displays - Include displays inside and out of the vehicles.

Traffic Count - The number of vehicles that pass a given location each day.

Transit Advertising - Refers to advertising displays attached to either moving vehicles or in areas where the public waits for transit such as buses, taxis, and airports.

Trim (Molding) - The frame that surrounds the surface (message) of a billboard – similar to a picture frame.

Tri-Vision - A painted display embellishment, which, through use of triangular louver construction, permits the display of three different messages in a pre-determined sequence. (Also called Multi-Vision).

Unit - A poster panel or painted bulletin

V-Type Sign - A sign structure that consists of multiple faces that are placed at angles to each other.

Wallscapes - Murals, paintings, or vinyls on the exterior of a building.

State Transportation Departments

Alabama Department of Transportation
1409 Coliseum Boulevard
P.O. Box 303050
Montgomery, Alabama 36130-3050
334-242-6358
www.tdot.state.tn.us

Alaska Department of Transportation & Public Facilities
Office of the Commissioner
3132 Channel Drive
PO Box 112500
Juneau, AK 99811-2500
907) 465-3901
www.dot.state.ak.us

Arizona Department of Transportation
205 South 17th Avenue, MD 612E
Phoenix, AZ 85007
(602) 712 - 7316
FAX
(602) 712 - 3257
www.dot.state.az.us/

Arkansas Department of Transportation
P.O. Box 2261
Little Rock, Arkansas 72203
501-569-2000
www.ahtd.state.ar.us

California Department of Transportation
1120 N Street Room 2221 (MS-52)

Sacramento, CA 95814
Telephone: (916) 654-4245
FAX: (916) 653-2134
www.dot.ca.gov/

Colorado Department of Transportation
4201 E. Arkansas Avenue
Denver, CO 80222
303-757-9011
www.dot.state.co.us

Connecticut Department of Transportation
2800 Berlin Turnpike
Newington, CT 06131-7546
www.ct.gov/dot

Delaware Department of Transportation
800 Bay Road , P.O. Box 778
Dover, DE 19903
302-760-2080 or 800-652-5600
www.deldot.net

District Department of Transportation
2000 14th Street, NW, 6th Floor
Washington, DC 20009
(202) 673-6813
www.ddot.dc.gov/main.shtm

Florida Department of Transportation
605 Suwannee Street
Tallahassee, Florida 32399-0450
(850) 414-4100
www.dot.state.fl.us/

Georgia Department of Transportation
No. 2 Capitol Square, S.W.
Atlanta, Georgia 30334
(404) 656-5267
(404) 463-6336 Fax
www.dot.state.ga.us/

Hawaii Department of Transportation
Aliiaimoku Building
869 Punchbowl Street
Honolulu, HI 96813
www.state.hi.us/dot

Idaho Transportation Department
3311 W. State Street · P.O. Box 7129
Boise, ID 83707-1129
208) 334-8000
www.itd.idaho.gov/

Illinois Department of Transportation
2300 S. Dirksen Pkwy.
Springfield, IL 62764
(217) 782-7820
www.dot.state.il.us

Indiana Department of Transportation
100 N. Senate Ave. Room IGCN 755
Indianapolis, IN 46204
Phone: (317) 232-5533
www.ai.org/dot/

Iowa Department of Transportation
800 Lincoln Way
Ames, IA 50010

Telephone: 515-239-1101
Fax: 515-239-1639
www.dot.state.ia.us

Kansas Department of Transportation
Dwight D. Eisenhower State Office Building
700 S.W. Harrison Street
Topeka, KS 66603-3754
785) 296-3566
www.ksdot.org/

Keytucky Department of Transportation
200 Mero Street, Mail Code E6-S1-00
Frankfort, KY 40622
Phone: 502-564-3730
Fax: 502-564-2277
www.kytc.state.ky.us

Louisiana Department of Transportation
Red River Waterway Commission
5941 Highway 1 Bypass
Natchitoches, LA 71457-2625
318-352-7446
www.dotd.state.la.us/

Maine Department of Transportation
Child Street
16 State House Station
Augusta, ME 04333-0016
(207) 624-3000
Fax (207) 624-3001
www.state.me.us/mdot

Maryland Department of Transportation
7201 Corporate Center Dr.
Hanover, Md. 21076
888-713-1414
www.mdot.state.md.us

Massachusetts Highway Department
10 Park Plaza, Suite 3170
Boston, MA 02116
TEL: (617) 973-7800
FAX: (617) 973-8040
www.magnet.state.ma.us/mhd/home.htm

State Transportation Department
425 W. Ottawa St.
P.O. Box 30050
Lansing, MI 48909
517-373-2090
www.michigan.gov/mdot/

Minnesota Department of Transportation
Central Office
Transportation Building
395 John Ireland Boulevard
Saint Paul, MN 55155
Phone: 651-296-3000
www.dot.state.mn.us/

Mississippi Department of Transportation
P.O. Box 1850
Jackson, MS 39215-1850
601) 359-7001
www.mdot.state.ms.us/

Missouri Department of Transportation
Central Office
105 W. Capitol Avenue
Jefferson City, MO 65102
1-888 ASK MODOT
(1-888 275 6636)
www.modot.state.mo.us

Montana Department of Transportation
2100 W Broadway
PO Box 7039
Missoula, MT 59807-7039
Phone: 406.523.5800
Fax: 406.523.5801
www.mdt.mt.gov/

Nebraska Department of Transportation
1500 Hwy. 2, P.O. Box 94759
Lincoln, NE 68509-4759
402-479-4512
www.dor.state.ne.us

Nevada Department of Transportation
1263 South Stewart Street
Carson City, Nevada 89712
Telephone: 775-888-7000
Fax: 775-888-7115
www.nevadadot.com/

New Hampshire Department of Transportation
John O. Morton Building
7 Hazen Drive
Concord, NH

03302-0483
Telephone: (603) 271-3734
Fax: (603) 271-3914
www.state.nh.us/dot/

Department of Transportation
P.O. Box 600
Trenton, NJ 08625-0600
www.state.nj.us/transportation/

New Mexico Department of Transportation
Bokum Building
142 West Palace Ave
2nd Floor
P.O. Box 1269
Santa Fe, New Mexico 87501
www.nmshtd.state.nm.us

New York State Department of Transportation
3407 State Route 3614855
Jasper, NY
607-792-3387
www.dot.state.ny.us

North Carolina State Department of Transportation
1500 Mail Service Center,
Raleigh NC, 27699-1500
919-733-2520
www.dot.state.nc.us

North Dakota Department of Transportation
608 East Boulevard Avenue
Bismarck, ND 58505-0700

701-328-2500
www.dot.nd.gov/

Ohio Department Of Transportation
1980 W. Broad St
Columbus, Ohio, 43223
Www.dot.state.oh.us

Oklahoma Department of Transportation
200 N. E. 21st Street
Oklahoma City, OK 73105
405- 521–2001
www.okladot.state.ok.us/

Oregon Department of Transportation
355 Capitol St. NE
Salem OR 97301-3871
888-ASK-ODOT
www.odot.state.or.us/

Pennsylvania Department of Transportation
Keystone Building
400 North Street
Harrisburg, PA 17120
General Information: 717-787-2838
www.dot.state.pa.us/

Rhode Island department of Transportation
Two Capital Hill
Providence, RI 02903
401-222-6510
http://www.dot.state.ri.us/publications/

South Carolina Department of Transportation
Attention: OSOW Permit Office

P.O. Box 191
Columbia, SC 29202
877- 349-7190
www.dot.state.sc.us/

South Dakota Department of Transportation
Aberdeen Region Office
PO Box 1767
Aberdeen, SD 57402-1767
605-626-2244

Pierre Region Office Rapid City Region Office
104 S. Garfield
Pierre, SD 57501
605-773-3464

Mitchell Region Office
PO Box 1206
Mitchell, SD 57301-7206
605-995-8129

Rapid City Region Office
PO Box 1970
Rapid City, SD 57709-1970
605-394-2244
www.sddot.com

Tennessee Department of Transportation
James K. Polk Building
505 Deaderick Street Suite 700
Nashville, TN 37243-0349
Phone: 615.741.2848
www.tdot.state.tn.us/

Texas Department of Transportation
125 East 11th Street
Austin, Texas 78701
512-416-2901
www.dot.state.tx.us/

Utah Department of Transportation
4501 South 2700 West
Mail Stop 141200
Salt Lake City, UT 84114-1200
801-965-4000
www.sr.ex.state.ut.us

Vermont Department of Transportation
One National Life Drive
Montpelier, VT 05633-5001
802-828-5324
www.aot.state.vt.us

Virginia Department of Transportation
VDOT Annex Bldg.
1401 E. Broad Street, 11th floor
Richmond, Virginia 23219
804-786-4871
www.virginiadot.org

Washington State Department of Transportation
Transportation Building
310 Maple Park Avenue SE
PO Box 47300
Olympia WA 98504-7300
360-705-7000
www.wsdot.wa.gov/

West Virginia Department of Transportation
Building 5
1900 Kanawha Blvd, East
Charleston WV, 25305-0330
Phone: 304-558-2822
Fax: 304-558-0454
www.wvdot.com/

Wisconsin Department of Transportation
4802 Sheboygan Avenue - Room 501
Madison WI 53702
608- 266-3813
www.dot.state.wi.us

Wyoming Department of Transportation
5300 Bishop Blvd
Cheyenne, WY 82009-3340
307-777-4375
www.dot.state.wy.us

(Initial Letter to Landowner)

This is a proposal to lease nine square feet of groundspace on your property fronting_____

_____ for the purpose of constructing and operating a high-quality outdoor advertising billboard sign.

As payment, you will receive $_____ per year with not time, effort or risk on your part.

Through proper position, the sign will not interfere in any way with the operation or aesthetics of your property.

Please call me at _____ to discuss this proposal. I look forward to hearing from you.

Sincerely,

_____

PHOTO OF WHERE THE SIGN WOULD GO
(if you have one)

Sign Location Lease

_____, the owner
of hereinafter described real property ("Lessor").

Hereby leases to _____
_____, a corporation ("Lessee"), a site outline and described on
Exhibit A to this Lease (the "Leased Premises"), for the purpose of
operating an outdoor advertising sign ("The Sign"), under the following terms and conditions:

1. This Lease is for a term of _____(___) years com-
   mencing on the date of execution. At Lessee's sole option,
   Lessee may renew this lease for an additional term of _____
   _____(___) years by written notice to Lessor not later than
   thirty (30) days before the expiration of the initial term.

2. The rent to be paid for the initial term and for any renewal
   term will be _____. The rent for the
   full initial term is payable in advance on the date of execution of this Lease. The rent for the full renewal term is payable in advance at the time notice or renewal is given.

3. Lessor agrees not to permit any obstruction located on any
   property owned by him to partially or completely obscure
   the normal highway view of the Sign. Lessee is hereby autho-
   rized at its option to remove any such obstruction.

4. Lessee agrees to maintain the Sign in a clean and sightly
   condition.

5. Lessee agrees to defend, indemnify, and hold Lessor harmless
   from and against any and all actions, cost, claims, losses, expenses, or damages made against or suffered by Lessor attrib-
   utable to or arising out of the negligent operation of the Sign
   by Lessee. Lessee agrees to procure and keep in effect during

the term of this Lease bodily injury and property damage liability insurance, with liability limits of $500,000 per person and $1,000,000 per occurrence. Lessor shall have no responsibility to Lessee for the security, installation, maintenance, or removal of the Sign or its appurtenances, except in the event of his or his agent's or employee's willful, reckless, negligent, or grossly negligent conduct.

6. Lessor represents and warrants that he has the authority to execute and deliver this Lease and that this Lease does not violate or cause a default under any deed of trust, mortgage, other lease, or any other agreement or instrument.

7. Lessor represents and warrants that he has fee simple title to the Leased Premises, free and clear of all liens, encumbrances, and other leases.

8. Any notice required or permitted by the Lease shall be given in writing and shall be deemed to be delivered if given in person or, whether or not actually received, when deposited in the United States mail, postage prepaid, certified mail, return receipt requested, addressed as set forth below or to such other address as the party to whom notice is to be sent has given ten (10) days' advance written notice.

9. In the event either party defaults in the performance of any of its obligations under this Lease and fails to cure such default within fifteen (15) days after notice of default has been delivered by the non-defaulting party shall have the right to terminate this Lease and/or pursue any other rights or remedies he or it may have against the defaulting party.

10. This Lease shall bind and inure to the benefit of the parties and their respective assigns, heirs, executors, representatives,

and successors, including any subsequent owner of the Lease Premises. This Lease shall be fully assignable by either party without the consent of the other part.

EXECUTED this _____day of March, 2007.

_____

Lessor

Address:_____

_____

_____

Lessee

By:_____

Vice-President

Address:_____

_____

STATE OF   §

　　　　　　　　　§

　　　　　　　　　§

This instrument was acknowledged before me on _____,
_____, by

_____

Notary Public in and for the State of

STATE OF   §

　　　　　　　　　§

§

This instrument was acknowledged before on _____,
_____,by _____, Vice-President of
_____, A corporation, on behalf of said
corporation.

_____

Notary Public in and for the State of

An Advertisement

THE BEST ADVERTISING VALUE IN THE LOVE FIELD/PARK CITIES MARKET.

REACHING OVER 30,000 OF YOUR POTENTIAL CUSTOMERS EACH DAY!

OUR BILLBOARD ON INWOOD ROAD BETWEEN MAPLE AVE. AND DENTON DRIVE

LOCATION: AT 2711 Inwood Road, between Maple Avenue and Denton Drive. North-bound, left-hand read.

TRAFFIC: Over 30,000 viewers each day.

SIZE: Large 10' x 40' advertising face, 50' high.

LIGHTING: Bright lighting at night.

COST: Only $695 per month including all artwork, painting, lighting and maintenance of your advertisement. This giant 50' tall salesman reaches over 900,000 of your potential customers each month on a salary of only $23 per day.

FOR MORE INFORMATION CONTACT FRANK ROLFE, SALES AGENT, AT (214)750-8637.

Making Money in Billboards: A Case Study, My Best 50 Deals and What Made Them Great.

By Frank Rolfe

July 12, 2007

Forward

I'm a big history buff, and I read mostly biographies and books on warfare. What makes it fun to read these things is to gather the lessons learned by many famous and successful people and overlay what worked for them on top of your own life plan. After you've read a lot of these books, you start to see certain patterns emerge that seem to show signs that an idea or action is going to be successful and, similarly, what actions do not appear to be good ideas if you want to win.

I wrote this book to give real-life examples of what seems to be the pattern for success in building a billboard company. All of these case studies are true stories, and all of the lessons learned happened to me. Not that I'm the only guy who has made big money in billboards – just the only one who seems to want to write about it!

So let's get started and begin to identify what works and what doesn't work in successful billboard deals.

Introduction

The following deals are all true stories; they show the wide range of niches that are required to cobble together a billboard operation of any size.

I have tried to include a section on lessons learned on each deal. You will have to notice that it reads like a broken record, because the same basic ideas keep popping up time after time. These are the key points you need to focus on.

When I got in the business, I thought it would all be about building cookie-cutter signs on the freeways, and then leasing the space. I had no idea how competitive it was. There were 60 billboard companies in my market. The competition was crazy. To survive, and prosper, you had to have a gimmick.

These stories represent my clever ideas on how to do deals in a competitive market. The fact that I could pull one of these off on average each month for fifteen straight years shows how many "outside the box" game plans I could dream up.

These formulas will give you a much greater chance for success than any other avenue.

I have included dollar amounts when appropriate, to show you the real-life returns that can be attained.

I think that if you study each deal carefully, you may identify a deal in your market that meets the same criteria, and you can copy my plans with enthusiasm.

Good luck and good hunting!

Frank Rolfe

An Amazing Deal that Anybody Could Have Had

Although I spent my career in the Dallas/Ft. Worth, Texas market, one of my greatest deals happened in Los Angeles, California.

It all began with an ad we were running that said "We Buy Billboards". The caller was a guy who had inherited about 24 billboard units in Los Angeles when his brother was killed in a car wreck. This guy had no idea how to run a billboard company, so he stopped taking calls, paying ground rents, and let all the ads go empty. He saw my ad and was intrigued.

He threw out a price and I accepted it at full price because it sounded low. The important part to me was what he agreed to… allowing me a six month diligence period to try and re-paper the ground leases.

When I flew out to L.A., I found that the locations were pretty decent with three of them standouts. The risk management part of my brain went to full speed, and I quickly decided to try and sell these three standout locations to a big billboard company to reduce my investment in the remaining signs. So I packed up these three signs (after renegotiating their ground leases) and met with the biggest sign companies in L.A. My hunch was a good one, because the biggest company offered me as much for the three signs as I was paying for the whole operation: $250,000.

What made this an amazingly great deal was the fact that I didn't have to put one cent into buying these signs. I did a simultaneous closing of the three signs and the entire operation. In one day I had gone from no signs in California, to a major player in Los Angeles and I had not risked one penny.

I found that operating billboards in L.A. was extremely difficult, and after a few years, I sold the L.A. operation off for a $300,000 profit. That amount was not very impressive, except for the fact that I had not one dollar in the deal.

And why hadn't the big local company contacted the guy directly to buy the signs before he ever called me? I ask them that after closing, and they said that they didn't want the other signs, only the three and the guy would not just sell the three by themselves. Now you may ask, why didn't they buy the whole group and sell off all but three signs and have no money in those three? Chalk that up to the amazing dynamics of big companies.

☒ THE LESSONS LEARNED HERE WERE:

- Thinking outside the box is very profitable

- Buying a group of assets and selling a few off to pay down debt is a great strategy.

- Big companies can make stupid decisions

YOU CAN MAKE MORE THAN WOODEN NICKELS OUT OF TELEPHONE POLES

This deal was strange from start to finish, but was a case study in risk management.

There was an abandoned wooden "telephone pole" billboard on a major highway outside of Dallas. I found the property owners name through the tax records and wrote them a letter asking if I could take over the abandoned sign and start paying them ground rent. Nobody responded. So, having their mailing address, I started dropping by their house. It was a big estate, with a maid in full uniform who answered the door. She would always take my business card, but still nobody ever called. After about three drop-bys, I got a call from the property owner. He basically said… what do you want? I told him and he said "here's the deal, I'll sign your lease if you promise never to come by my house again, or even contact me – because you scare me" He thought I was some type of stalker or something.

I spent about $2,000 fixing the sign up and then rented it immediately to homebuilders. Over time, the net income grew to a pretty consistent $20,000 per year, all on a $2,000 investment. If the sign had blown down in a storm (which old telephone pole signs do all the time) I would have only been out $2,000 – but I made that back in the first two months.

Where else can you get a return like that? Nowhere that I've ever seen.

When I sold the sign years later, I got $60,000 for it. So the total income from that $2,000 was something like $260,000.

The lesson learned here was again the beauty of having very low capital in a sign deal, and refusing to give up in getting the sign lease.

THINKING OUTSIDE THE BOX MAKES MONEY AGAIN

The father of one of my landowners had an unusual situation. He had literally won an old, abandoned billboard in a card game. What made it tough to utilize was that the sign, instead of one big face, had three sections to it. It basically had three rectangles of ad space separated by about 4' between each section.

I leased the structure from him, along with a long-term ground lease.

I used the odd configuration as a marketing weapon. I proposed that someone rent the sign that could us the middle panel to advertise periodic sales and such.

I found an auto parts store that put there name on the top panel, the address on the bottom panel, and a product on sale on the middle. Then they were able to get the company that made that product to pay part of the cost for the billboard as a coop. This advertiser stayed on the sign for the duration that I owned it. The three panel side formation had tuned into a unique product that only we had to offer.

I put about $7,000 into reconfiguring the sign, and it made about $12,000 per year. When I sold it in 1996, I received about $60,000 for it. The stream of income summed to about $180,000.

☒ **THE LESSON LEARNED WAS:**

- Think outside the box for success
- You can't beat having a low amount of equity in a deal because it makes your return on investment enormous, and your downside risk insignificant.

THE STUPIDEST DEAL EVER – FOR THE SELLER

I had a regular routine of calling the big billboard companies about once per month to see if they had any junk to sell off. I was looking for billboard signs, preferably decent locations, but often I would buy used panels and lights and such.

One day, the guy tells me that they have a billboard that has been vacant for three years, and they are tired of paying ground rent on it. They offer it to me for $10,000 – and they'll carry the paper for three years.

Then they gave the location and I almost passed out. It was right smack in downtown Dallas and 14' x 48' in size. I drove on out and saw immediately what the problem was. There was a premise sign for a car lot right smack in the middle of it.

I tied it up under contract, and then met with the car lot owner. Without any effort they agreed to lower their sign if I would pay for it. It turns out that they never wanted the sign that high to begin with. So I spent $1,000.00 to lower their sign and I had a spectacular billboard with almost no capital in it.

☒ *LESSON LEARNED:*

- If I haven't said it enough already; think outside the box. Why had the big company not approached the car lot? I have no idea.

- There's no better situation than a billboard with almost no capital in it.

- Big companies throw away treasures all the time, and if you can put yourself in a position to "sort through their trash" then you can get some unbelievable deals. As an aside, I once rented a truck and went to Houston to pick up the junk panels from a big billboard company. By my standards they were nearly new, and they charged me about $200 for the load, about 90% fair market value.

- The big company blows it again

ANOTHER BIG COMPANY MISTAKE

A big billboard company has a 14' x 48' two sided unit on a major freeway and is unsuccessful in renting it on a consistent basis. The sales force tells management that it has a short read, but really the reason is they just don't want to work it properly. And it's got a read short enough that nobody calls them asking to rent it

They try to renegotiate the ground rent. The lesser tells them no, but that he'll buy it if it's so lousy.

They agree and the billboard now belongs to the ground owner. I hear about the change, and go to the landowner and offer to pay him $20,000 for the sign and also pay him an immediate $400 per month ground rent. He takes my offer without any negotiation.

In effect, I have bought about $40,000 of steel, panels and lights for 50% off, not counting the value of the lease and permit. The location was on a major highway on the edge of downtown.

I sold the unit in 1996 for about $100,000. And did I mention that the sign made a 50% return on the $20,000 every year prior to the sale.

- The lesson learned here was that big companies do make mistakes. That's why you need to keep a continual conversation going with all of them offering to buy their "dog" signs. And when you see a new phone number go up on a sign, call immediately and see if they want to sell the sign. You'll find that most people do not really want to be in the billboard business, and are more than happy to sell the asset to you cheap.

THE BIG COMPANY CAN'T STOP BLOWING IT

A big billboard company decides to terminate the lease on a 14' x 48' billboard because they can't rent the space. They try to go out and cut the billboard down, but the property owner sues them saying that the lease does not allow for removal of the sign. Rather than pay legal fees, they just give him the sign.

Driving by one day, I see a new phone number go up on the sign, so I call it, and reach an elderly retired CPA who is the new owner of the sign but really doesn't want to be.

It turns out that he owns only the little piece of land under the sign, and bought the little piece for the billboard income. All he wants is the income like he was getting before.

I propose to immediately go back to giving him his billboard ground rent, and he agrees to sell me the sign structure for $10,000 – and he'll carry the paper!

The reason the big company could not rent the billboard was tree obstructions on the east-bound read. Apparently, nobody had ever tried to fix the problem, only complain about it. I went to the owner of the neighboring property that had the trees, and without any compensation he told me to go trim or chop whatever I wanted.

I trimmed the trees and had both sides rented almost immediately.

I later sold this sign for about $100,000 – and had no money in the deal, due to the owner financing.

- The lesson learned here is the same as last one. Big companies can be pretty stupid, so keep a communication channel going to buy their "junk" and whenever you see a new phone number go up on a sign, call it ASAP and see if it's an opportunity.

I'LL TAKE $70,000 WITH THAT ORDER OF FRIES PLEASE

Terry's was a chain of burger restaurants which had a successful run for several decades during the initial construction of the interstate highway system. However, with the advent of McDonalds and other chains, particularly with drive-thru windows versus Terry's strictly dine-in format, sales plunged and ultimately most of the units closed down. There was, however, one asset that Terry's had that nobody thought of. And that was all those old billboards that now carried valuable permits, scattered up and down the highway.

When I approached Terry's about buying the billboards (the original founder was still alive), he thought I was nuts. Who would want to buy a bunch of old, rotten signs? As a result, the sales price was very reasonable – about $2,000 per unit.

The next trick was getting in good with the landowners again. Terry's sign leases had very small ground lease amounts – some as low as $50 per year. It didn't take more than $1,000 per sign to catch up the past ground rents and re-paper a new, modern lease. The permits were still in fine condition, having no expiration date.

Now that I had about $3,000 in each sign, I began to inventory what was needed to get them back in service. Thank God for telephone poles, because the poles were all fine. All I had to do was install new stringers and sign faces. That was quick and easy, and I started renting the billboard faces. Due to their great locations, and especially the fact that they only had one sign – the one on the right hand side going toward town, they rented easily.

My $3,000 investment per sign grew to about $5,000 after the new face. My $5,000 investment returned about $3,000 per year. After about seven years, I sold them for about $10,000 each. In effect, my $5,000 investment had returned about $31,000 each. In broader terms, my $35,000 investment for seven signs had yielded $217,000. Over seven years that's about a 600% return. I think that's better than the stock market during the same period, but I'm not sure.

CAN I HAVE THAT SAME ORDER AGAIN

After my success with the Terry's signs, I decided to make a run at the old abandoned Stuckey's signs in east Texas.

For those of you who do not know what Stuckey's is, it was a major franchise of restaurants, and sometimes gasoline throughout most of the United States. There may be some signs like these left in your market, so pay careful attention.

It was a challenge finding the decision maker for a group of old wooden sighs, but I finally found the owner in Atlanta. Just like Terry's they had no idea why someone would want them. But unlike Terry's, they had a board of directors and a very slow bureaucratic process. It became a battle of perpetual procrastination. Calling Stuckey's became a part of my regular workweek. Every Monday I would call and get a million excuses as to why they had not yet made a decision.

About a year went by, and suddenly one Monday they said they had decided to sell them to me. But, of course, that then meant that I had to wait for a contract. And wait. And wait. About six months later they were ready to sign up. To save myself from the delay of shipping the documents out, I went to Atlanta to sign up. And I have to say that the law office we met at was spectacular – the top floor of the tallest office building in Atlanta. But what I couldn't figure out was how there would be any money after legal fees for Stuckey's.

Once I had the signs, it was the same process as Terry's. Renegotiate ground rents, re-paper leases, verify the permits were good, and re-face the signs. The economics proved out to be the same as Terry's, which made sense since they were all on the same highway.

- The lessons learned here were that there is good money in resuscitating dead signs, and that you have to be persistent. I think that most everyone else would have given up, or taken their perpetual lack of action as a "no".

How I Turned the Tables on a Liar and Made an Even Better Deal

When I started working the Denton, Texas market, there was one location that I decided would be the most important one in the market if it could be secured. It was right in the middle of a big curve in the highway, and the visibility of this sign would be unequaled. The property owner was a car dealer. I would like to point out that I have never had a good experience doing anything with a car dealer, so I should have known better.

I met with the guy, and he told me that if I could rent the ads first, to prove to him that the sign would be occupied by quality businesses, that he would sign my lease. So I went about leasing the ad space for a sign "to be built" and about ninety days later I went back to the car dealer, with the ad leases in hand. He looked them over and then told me that he really was going to build the sign with a buddy of his, but thanks for renting the ads for them. I was determined, at that moment, to get even with him. So when I pulled out of his parking lot, I headed for the Texas Transportation office where you file sign permit applications. You see, I already had had the application ready when I went to the meeting. And all I had to do was move my location sketch over about 50' and I would be on the neighbor's land. And the neighbor's name I knew from the ownership records.

When I got to the highway department office, I used their phone to call the neighbor. I explained the situation, and he gave me his O.K. to pull the permit. So I made my application on the neighbor's property. Meanwhile, little did I know that the car dealer and his buddy were right behind me, heading down to file their permit. They also had theirs ready, but had held off filing it until I did their work for them in renting the ad faces. By the time they got there, the location was mine, and they were screwed.

I rented the billboard to a beer company, and they renewed the billboard year-after-year for about 20 years. The sign cost $50,000 to build, and sold for $150,000 fourteen years later.

- The moral to this story is never give up. Until the movie's over, anything can still happen. I myself could not believe that I pulled that deal off.

A side note for those who enjoy stories of divine retribution. A few years later, the Texas economy went bust, and the car dealer went bankrupt. All of his kids, who he employed in the dealership, were fired when it closed down. And the guy who had tried to screw me died of a heart attack right in the middle of it all. That may make even the staunchest atheist reconsider.

A SUDDEN TURN OF FORTUNE ONLY GETS BETTER

After I built the billboard on the neighbors' land, he mentioned that he had another parcel farther down the highway. I measured it, and it was a legal location. He signed my lease, I pulled the permit, and that became my second sign in Denton.

It was just that easy.

- The lesson learned is that landowners often own more than one piece of land. Ask them where their other pieces are, and then see if they are legal locations.

After this deal, I would always ask an owner what other pieces of land they owned, and on several occasions it resulted in additional billboard deals.

This second sign cost about $40,000 to build and I sold it for around $100,000 years later.

ANOTHER BIG COMPANY GONE STUPID

As you probably realize by now, I am always calling competitors to see if they have any "dog" assets they want to sell really cheap. This time, they called me.

There was a 106" x 36' two-sided monopole billboard in a blighted area of town. It had been empty for years, and the sales force was too scared to even call on customers down there.

They called me and wanted to sell me the sign for $1,000. Just think of how stupid that alone is. The structure, lights and panels are worth maybe $20,000. But the bottom line is that it's not their money, and they don't want to mess with a sign in the bad part of town.

Sure, I took the billboard for $1,000 and started making the $200 per month ground rent. But I changed the ad sales strategy. Instead of trying to sell the sign to businesses in the bad area, I made a list of businesses in the good area that sell to the bad area. The most logical choice was attorneys. So I did a mass mailing to all of the law firms in the city, and the next thing you know, I've rented the sign for full asking price to an attorney – advertising "I can get you out of jail". If that had failed, I'm sure I could have rented it to a bail bondsman, or something like that.

The $1,000 sign made $5,000 of profit per year. And in 1996, I sold it for $40,000. Over a six year period, the $1,000 had grown to $70,000.

The moral here is:

- Keep in continual contact with your competitors

- Think outside the box on everything you do. If something is not working, don't give up. Just take a new direction and try again.

I bet in the market you're in, there are signs in blighted areas that you could use this same strategy on. I even used it on some bad areas in Los Angeles, and it worked great there too.

NOW A SMALL COMPANY GETS STUPID TOO

Do you ever drive by vacant billboards, ones that have been vacant for years, and wonder what the heck is going on? Then this story is for you.

I noticed a billboard on a lesser highway that was always vacant, year after year. I knew the owner, so I called to see if it was for sale. He told me he'd give it to me for $1 if I could get him out of his obligations. It seems that he'd had a cash flow problem at one time, and didn't pay the guy his rent. He hadn't paid him in about three years. Since he owed the guy so much money, about $21,000, he was too afraid to go on the property to rent and paint the sign.

So the deal was that I could buy it for $1 if I could produce a document saying the ground rent was paid up to date and that he didn't owe a penny more after closing.

Of course, the first questions might be why didn't he sell the sign for $40,000, pay the guy off, and keep the profit. I guess the answer is that he would have to get estoppels prior to closing, and could not float the $21,000 between estoppels and closing.

So, I call the guy up and I get the first big shock – he doesn't own the property anymore. He lost it to foreclosure by the bank. That explains why he wasn't pressing on the billboard guy any harder.

So I called the bank, and got shock number two – the bank has failed and been taken over by government regulators (this was during the 1980's savings and loan crisis). So they refer me on to the U.S. Government. When I reach the guy at the government, he is excited to think that there is a source of $7,000 per year in income on the vacant land, and wants to get the ground rent going immediately. So he agrees to forgive the past amount owed.

I get it in writing and close on the sign for $1.

As you can guess, the seller tries to renege, since I didn't have to pay a penny out of pocket (beside the $1). However, I have the deal in writing and he realizes that he'll lose in court, so he goes ahead with it.

☒ *THE LESSONS LEARNED ARE:*

- Always get your deals in writing. Always.

- Don't be afraid to take on impossible projects, as long as you have no money at risk, because sometimes things go your way.

- Don't get behind on your ground rent. More than anyone else, you need that landowner happy.

THE CRAZY STORY OF BILLCO

My Billco deal was my first large acquisition of multiple signs from one owner. It had so many cliffhangers that it was great training for every deal to come later, because if I ever thought it was a done deal, I was proved wrong by the next day.

The deal began with a call on a vacant billboard to see if they would sell. They never called back. I kept calling, but they never called back. So I asked around and got the name of the owner, who had a roofing company. So I went over to the roofing company, and soon learned why they wouldn't call me back. It turns out that the original owner had run off and deeded the billboards to his mother. Since she had no idea how to run a billboard company, she had gone into a "hide from everyone" mode and tried to forget about the signs. She also had not paid the bank – I think ever.

My deal with her was that I would buy all of the signs for $1 plus what I had to pay the bank to get her out of the loan she was in default on.

Step one was that she gives me 120 days to get all of the ground leases fixed.

Bear in mind that she had not been paying any of the landowners, so I had a real challenge. Also, I was asking them to sign new leases that only took effect if I closed on the deal – not much of an offer. Unbelievably, within 120 days I had solved all of the leases and they were signed.

The permits were all O.K. and a non- issue.

Now came the hard part, settling with the bank.

The bank had failed and was now if the hands of the FDIC. So I called the FDIC and made what I thought was a reasonable offer. They told me it was ridiculous, that they wanted the full amount of the loan (about $500,000) or forget it.

So after all of my hard work, it looked like I had nothing to show for my effort. The signs were only worth to me about $150,000, so we were clearly way too far apart on price.

I was very disappointed, but I moved on. I kept calling Billco every week to see if there was any new development that might go my way.

Then suddenly, there was a break. The FDIC had filed to go into mediation on the loan. I asked if I could attend the mediation and they said "why not".

At mediation, you basically have both parties in separate rooms, and the mediator moves between rooms making offers back and forth. I was in the room with the Billboard Company or debtor.

The mediator came in at about 9 am and said that the FDIC wanted $500,000. The Debtor said she had no money or assets except for a used Cadillac. So he left the room.

Later he came back and offered $400,000. Again, she said it was not a negotiating ploy – she really had no money.

He kept coming back with new numbers, $350,000, $300,000, $250,000. Apparently the FDIC thought she really had money and was just negotiating them.

Finally, near 5 pm, he came in with the offer of $150,000. This was their final offer. She told him again that she was broke. So he turned to me and asked "Why are you here?" I told him that I was with a billboard company and we might be interested in buying the signs. How much? He asked. I said $60,000. He left the room again.

In twenty minutes he came back in. "Here's the deal, you pay $60,000 (pointing to me) and you pay us $200 a month for two years (pointing to her). She turned to me and I said "take the deal and I'll cover your $200". So the deal was struck.

Now, you might ask, why did the FDIC not take my initial offer for $150,000 months earlier? And why did they not remember that offer when they settled for $60,000? Just another example of how stupid big companies could be.

☒ THE LESSONS LEARNED WERE:

- Never give up
- Always look for the weak spot on the big company because they make lots of stupid mistakes
- No deal is done until it's over.

ONE OF MY MOST IMPORTANT DEALS THAT ALMOST BANKRUPTED ME TWICE

As you already probably figured out, I like to call on the phone numbers on signs that have been vacant for a long time and see if the owner wants to sell. My theory is that nobody has much affection for a billboard they can't rent.

So I called the owner of a small billboard operation in Dallas that had a ton of vacancies to see if he would sell. He said he might have an interest at the right price, so I put together an offer and arranged for a meeting.

Immediately, upon seeing my offer, he said that he wasn't interested – my price was too low. I asked him if, since I had spent so much time putting it together, we could go through my assumptions together so he could educate me more about the business. This is where I learned my new trick of letting the owner determine his own price. We went through my rent and cost assumptions and he couldn't find anything wrong with them. So he changed his mind – maybe it was the correct price after all. But, since he was a seller, and I a buyer, we had to do some negotiations anyway, so the final price was a little higher than my offer price.

With that in hand came the next obstacle. Almost all of the leases were pretty old and expired soon. I would have to renegotiate and extend the leases. So he gave me 120 days to get them extended, which I did.

Next came another big hurdle; getting the deal financed. I was still using my local bank and this deal exceeded their loan limit. So they sent it over to a bank they had a "reciprocal" arrangement with that was bigger and had a higher loan limit. After studying the deal, they agreed to make the loan.

On the day of closing the bank called. They had changed their mind -- they were not going to do the deal. They had suddenly got concerned over making a billboard loan when they had never done one before (can you see why I hate banks?). I explained that it was too late, they had already given me a commitment letter and closing was that day. They said tough luck. I asked to speak to their boss.

I told him the story and offered to sue them if they backed out, and promised that a jury would not find their story very satisfactory. I also reminded them that I would sue for some huge amount of damages for losing the deal and devote my life to driving them nuts. So the guy gave me a counter proposal – they would fund about 80% of the original promised loan amount. Of course, that meant that I would lose all of my liquidity, and not even have enough money to cover such items as my legal bill. But what choice did I have? So I agreed.

Immediately following closing, the new bind of having no money made everything miserable. I was on the razor's edge of going broke on a daily basis. I had to rob Peter to pay Paul, and ask everyone to give me a break. It was awful. This new acquisition was killing me.

However, the worst was yet to come. There were two billboards in the deal that had big rents and a lot of value – and a lot of risk. They were located out by the airport, and they were on railroad leases which are terminable at any time with 24 hours notice. I met with the railroad prior to closing and they assured me that the signs would be there forever. You guessed it – the railroad sent me a letter terminating the leases.

I drove down to the guy who told me that could never happen and he told me that the railroad had hired a new broker to sell off their unneeded land and this guy had decided to terminate the lease because the billboards made the land ugly. Then they told me to get out of their office.

These signs had been valued in the deal at $100,000 each – about 40% of the total deal cost. This was a nuclear disaster. I was certain that the bank would call my loan and I would be put in bankruptcy.

I had two strategies; one was to delay the sign's removal and the other was to come up with the two "decoy" signs to swap the bank as collateral. To delay the removal, I had our attorney file suit against the railroad just to buy time. The suit was completely frivolous except for the fact that they had completely lied to me and made assurances that weren't there. And then I hit the road, roller wheel in hand, to find two replacement locations.

My luck was with me on the ground lease side. I found two decent locations – although certainly not $100,000 locations. I convinced the sign builder to carry the papers so I could pay him off over time, with a little down payment from the cash I really didn't have. I built the locations immediately.

Meanwhile, my lawsuit was going nowhere and was certain to be tossed out. But at least it had bought me an extra month.

Now came the next hurdle: I had to convince the bank to swap the two $100,000 signs out of the package and replace them with two new weaker signs.

I decided the only hope was to send them a short letter (more like a note) announcing the swap and claiming it was a great deal for the bank. The trick worked because the big bank never even called me to ask what it was all about. It just slipped through the cracks. Meanwhile, I didn't need a lien release on the two structures coming down as I wasn't selling them, so I took them down and put them in a steel yard. (Later, when the loan was moved to a different bank, with the substitution complete, I sold them for scrap). The big bank never even noticed that they came down – they never really paid much attention to the loan anyway.

Now came the biggest hurdle. I had just lost my two largest earning signs. I had replaced them with low earning signs that had extra debt on them (the builder's pay-off), so they actually negatively cash-flowed. How would I pay the bills? The answer was a monumental step. I had only one cost to cut – personnel. I fired everyone at the company except the bookkeeper. I now had to do everything myself. But at least I had staved off bankruptcy.

Now where's the happy ending here? This all took place in 1988. There was no happy ending until 1996. When I sold these signs to Universal Outdoor, this group of signs formed my key nucleus of most attractive signs. The locations were all on major highways near downtown. It was these signs that really wowed them. So I have to credit this acquisition with the spectacular sale I made of all the signs. But to think they nearly killed me along the way. I had paid $550,000 for the signs and I sold them for around a $1,000,000 profit.

☒ THE LESSONS LEARNED FROM THIS DEAL WERE:

- Never give up

- Stay away from banks if you can help it – they will one day be your worst enemy (Courtesy Leasing, which I love, was not a bank)

- Think outside the box

- Let the owner establish his own price through doing the numbers with you

- Strategically think long-term. If you only think short term you'll be too afraid to do anything.

EARNINGS PER HOUR THAT RIVAL A SPORTS STAR

After selling out to the Universal Outdoor, I reviewed all of the areas that I had thought might yield locations. My deal had given Universal a first option on any billboard location I found for a period of years, so I thought I would tie up some leases and permits and sell it to them. At this point, I was so skilled in getting ground leases, that it took me only a weekend to find a bunch of possible locations. I signed up what I could and then pulled the permits.

With the leases and permits in hand, and a map of locations, I met with the Universal guys. I offered them the whole group at $15,000 per lease, and I had eight of them. They took it without counter offer.

The total price was $120,000. I had spent maybe 100 hours on the whole project. That works out to $1,200 per hour.

I don't know what sports stars make exactly, but that has to be right in the ballpark.

And my total investment was about $400 in permit fees. That's all I ever had at risk.

☒ *LESSONS LEARNED FROM THIS DEAL:*

- Flipping leases is fantastically profitable

- Anyone can flip leases if you know what you're doing.

- Many companies today focus on buying leases rather than hiring land men. This is a great time to flip leases!

A CLASSIC TEXTBOOK SIGN DEAL

This deal ia as close to textbook billboard 101 as you can find. It illustrates the correct construction for a deal and how the numbers normally turn out.

I found a location on a major Interstate highway, but about 20 miles outside of town. I built a 14' x 48', and it cost about $35,000. The rents were $500 per month and the ground rent was 20% of gross.

Over time the rent escalated, with the market, to $1,000 per month per face. It stayed rented 100% of the time to local users such as car dealers and motels.

The income was $7,000 per year when I built it (20% returns on total investment) and I put 20% down on a $35,000 loan, so my return on equity day on was over 40%.

Years later, at $1,000 per month, the net income was $16,000 per year, and the returns had more than doubled.

I sold the sign after 12 years for about $80,000

The total return on my $7,000 investment was $_____.

⊠ *LESSONS LEARNED FROM THIS DEAL:*

- This is the textbook construction for a good billboard investment.

- If you follow this construction, you can never go wrong and will make lots of money.

Thinking Outside The Box Scores A Home Run

There was a great location on a major highway in Dallas that nobody could get a lease on, because on the property stood a new, upscale apartment building.

The owner was not going to let a billboard hurt the looks of his new complex.

So I sent a proposal to the owner that included a unique feature, the pole of the billboard would be covered in brick to match his apartment building.

The guy called me out of curiosity because he didn't think it could be done. I assured him that I talked to a brick mason, and it was possible to cover the steel column in matching brick – 40' high but only 4' in diameter. This idea intrigued him – plus he liked the $6,000 per year of ground rent angle.

As soon as I built the sign, the apartment owner liked it so much that he rented the billboard himself. So I had no sales cost or exposure as the sign advertised the apartments for as long as we owned it.

And as soon as I built this portfolio piece, I used photos of it to hit up the other properties that had aesthetic concerns like this one. From that I scored two more similar billboards.

⊠　***LESSONS LEARNED FROM THIS DEAL:***

- Think outside the box
- When you invest in something new, market it heavily
- Always remember that the business on your property may be a potential advertiser

How I Built A $10,000 14'X 48'

I had a location on an Interstate highway on raw land. The traffic count was good, but the neighborhood was pretty blighted and there were a fair amount of vacant signs in the immediate area. I ran the numbers, and with the level of vacancy and potential for low ad rents, the only way that I would have the guts to build it was if I could do it for $10,000.

Obviously that would seem impossible – but you know that I like to think outside the box. To make it happen, the key would be to find a way to build the metal structure really cheap, since that's about 90% of the construction tab.

I called around to all the local sign builders looking for scrap structures torn down from other locations, but they either had none or they had new monopolies slightly used for $20,000. Then I thought, "I wonder if I could cobble it together from scrap pieces at these guy's shops?"

So I called them all back again. One guy had the correct I-beams, and one guy had the angle iron. I asked around to see if any sign builder was slow on work at that particular time. I asked that guy if he could build a structure from I-beams and used angle iron for $8,000 including materials. He said he could.

Now the trick was to find panels and lights for $2,000. I knew that the cost to install the lights was $1,000, so I had only $1,000 to spend on parts. So I started calling all of the billboard companies in Texas to see if they had any scrap panels or light fixtures sitting in their yard that I could buy. Foster & Kleiser in Houston had scrap panels at $200 per face, so I rented a U-Haul and picked them up. That left me only $600 for light fixtures. I couldn't find any, but then I remembered that I saw light fixtures on some rural billboards that looked just like the 400 watt fixtures you see in Home Depot. They had an outdoor security light, 400 watt, for $100 per unit. I had never used them on a sign before but thought "why not?" Of course, they are lousy, since they have no lens or mirrors to focus the light, but would the advertiser really care in this instance.

Ultimately my $10,000 Frankenstein structure was erected and nobody ever complained about the lights. I sold this unit later for $40,000, which was a 400% return.

☒ *LESSONS LEARNED FROM THIS DEAL:*

- Think outside the box.
- I could have been lazy and bought a structure for full retail at $40,000, but I stuck to my guns and persevered. This made the economics correct, and made a marginal location a money-maker.

A City Council Gives Me A Location

Well, not actually a location. But they did give me the variance to build it. Here's how.

There was a town that did not allow billboards. But, there was this great sign location in the middle of a big curve in the highway. So I decided to try something that I knew had a low probability of success.

I went to the owner of the property, and signed up a lease contingent on getting approval from the city. I then went to the city and requested to be on the city council docket to request a variance to the sign ordinance to build a sign.

First I had to go to Planning and Zoning. They unanimously told me "no". They didn't even ask me any questions.

I told the owner, who was a long-time resident, and he was pretty mad that they said "no". So he started working on his friends on the city council.

I went to the council meeting and, again without asking any questions, they voted "yes". It made the local newspaper and the P&Z guys quit over it, saying the council didn't listen to them.

How did the landowner do it? I don't know. Obviously, he had a lot of pull in town.

Later on I had to meet him at his house. I had only met him at his office previously, which was in a run-down building. His house, however, was a mansion on top of a hill overlooking the town. Obviously, this guy had more going on that met the eye.

The strange ending was that, despite the great location, the town was so mad about the billboard that they basically boycotted the advertising on it. The sign performed O.K, and I sold it for a $20,000 profit down the road, but it was not the winner I had hoped. But, it was a thrilling adventure that mixed outdoor advertising with mob undertones.

☒ LESSONS LEARNED:

- Think outside the box.
- If a city says "no", ask for a variance – it might just happen.

ANOTHER BIG COMPANY SCREW UP

I got a call from a big company that had a "dog" sign that had been vacant for years. This time it scared me a little because it was very rural – but still on an interstate highway.

The price was right: $5,000 and they would finance it over two years.

The visibility was O.K. on one side, but had some tree obstructions the other way that I could not fix; the trees were on the highway right-of-way.

This was a battle of renting ad space, nothing more.

A big "for rent" on the billboard wouldn't help -- the big company had already tried that. So I did one of my mass mailings and I got a call and signed them up; it was a motel about 10 miles down the highway. But the other side wouldn't move at all.

Then I realized I had never called on the foreign auto parts business underneath the sign. It was a long shot, but what the heck. The guy really liked the idea. We installed an ad that just said "Foreign Auto Parts" and a big arrow aiming straight down.

The sign was never a big money maker, but sold for $30,000 in 1996 – the important point is that I had not one dollar in it! And that's why it was a winner in my mind.

☒ *LESSONS LEARNED:*

- Every sign can be rented, you just have to think outside the box

- Any sign you can get for $0 down is a winner.

I Build The Biggest Sign in Dallas – Barely

This was my first billboard and it was a good thing that I did not know what I was doing or I would never have had the guts to build it.

There was this great location on an Interstate highway. It had the right zoning and spacing. Why was there no sign on it? I didn't know, but I was the guy to do it.

I signed up a ground lease and decided to build the biggest sign in Dallas, a 20' x 60' x 120' tall sign. Why so big? I wasn't sure if I would ever find another location so I thought I might have to live off of just this one!

Everything went well until construction day. Then I realized the problem. The property was so small; there was no room to build the sign, only room for the fully erected sign to hang over.

I didn't figure this out until the semis full of steel arrived. They unloaded them on the property, and the pipe in segments. This steel covered the entire property. They started bolting and welding the head of the sign together. Once the head was assembled, they moved it over so that the auger driller could wedge in. Once the hole was drilled they put the pipe in.

Now came the time to put the head on – and there was no place to put the cranes on the property. The cranes would have to reach it form the neighbors land – the Texas Highway Patrol office.

Now I knew why nobody had built this location. The big companies saw that there was no access to build it and forgot about it. I didn't know any better, and had now put everything at risk with no possible solution.

I've always thought that if you need a cab ride, you should tell the cabby that you don't have any money after the ride if you really want to get there. I figured that if I could get the cranes on the neighbor's property and the head in the air, they couldn't stop me from bolting it on safely, and then they could yell at me all they wanted, but the sign would be up.

So I waited until lunch (you know how state troopers like to eat) and then I went to the receptionist and said that I needed to move a piece of equipment across their property to service the neighbor. I think she thought a lawn mower, not two 30 ton cranes.

No sooner had we brought the cranes across the parking lot and started lifting the head of the sign up, the cops started pouring out of the building. I looked back at the cranes and saw that in moving across the parking lot they had crushed and destroyed the asphalt and crushed the curb. I told the crane guys and the installation guys to keep going no matter what happened. The cops started yelling at me for wrecking their property without permission and I kept them yelling to buy time. I kept watching the sign to make sure that the head was on. Once the head was on, I was in business.

After yelling at me for about 20 minutes by various supervisors, I promised that I would fix the asphalt damage and never get on their property again.

What if they had stopped me before I got the head on? I would have been out of business big time.

This sign rented for $1,500 per month per side and was the talk of the east side of town for a long time. I sold it for about $120,000 in 1996.

☒ THE LESSONS LEARNED ARE:

- On property access issues, move first and ask permission later, if permission looks impossible

- Better lucky than smart

A Calculated Risk Goes Bad, Then Good Again

I had secured two leases and permits in a small town that fronted an Interstate highway.

After I had received the permit, but prior to building the signs, I got a letter form the city saying that they were retracting all of the permits – they didn't want any new signs.

Our attorney said that they could not retract them once issued, as long as I commence construction within 120 days, as allowed under the permit. But it was critical that I commenced construction. If I did not, then the old permit would die and they would not give me a new one.

So we went about building them on a weekend, figuring nobody would be around to stop us. Boy were we wrong. When the digger showed up the police stopped him and told him no signs could be built. So we went back again and he showed up again. So we called it a day and decided to try again at dawn, when the cop would be off-duty and not as energetic.

At dawn, nobody showed up, and we dug the sign. We put the pole in while still watching for cops or city officials. Then we got the concrete in, still unopposed.

The city figured out what was going on by the next day -- but you have to let the concrete cure before you put the head on. They threatened us, but we were determined to get the head on. We waited until city hall shut down, and then right before dark, the crane rolled in and the heads went on.

The city sent us a letter demanding we tear them down, but our attorney shot back that we had the legal right to build them and there was nothing they could do about it. He must have been right, because after a while, they never mentioned it again.

I sold these signs for a significant profit years later.

☒ *LESSONS LEARNED:*

- Once you get your sign in, it changes the whole playing field on shutting you down.

- Never be bullied by city hall. They often lie and they are not that smart.

- A competitor was too afraid to build his and let the permit lapse. If only he had had the guts to stand up to city hall.

THE MOST IMPOSSIBLE BILLBOARD DEAL EVER ACHIEVED BY MAN

What was I thinking? This was the most ridiculously impossible deal ever attempted, and I still can't believe I pulled it off.

There was a location in Lewisville, Texas that was fantastic. It was the intersection of two highways, and the sign could be seen by traffic on both highways at the same time, so it really had four different reads.

I got the ground lease, and then went down to get my permit. The city had a poison pill section in the sign ordinance. To get the permit, you had to get the written permission from every property owner within 200 feet. That meant I had to get written permission from a Waffle House, a shopping center, a car dealership, a motel, a Chili's, and a raw piece of land. If any of them refused, the deal was dead.

And I had nothing to offer them. I was proposing to build a big ugly sign that they would look out on and yet receive no cash compensation.

So I started meeting with them. I would never accept "no". I brown-nosed them, ate at their restaurant, begged, and pleaded, anything. I must have been insane. I devoted my life to it.

I finally convinced the motel to agree. Once I had their support, it makes the others a bit more willing, plus I was driving them all nuts with my drop-bys, letters and calls. If they said no I would say, please keep thinking about it and I'll be back.

After about six months I had all the approvals, and went to get my permit. The city freaked out, they could not believe that I had done it. They didn't think it was possible, and that's why they put it in the ordinance.

I got my permit and built the sign It was one of my best perform-ing signs, staying rented at all times for about $2,500 per month. It was about a 70% return on debt + equity.

☒ LESSONS LEARNED:

- Never take no for an answer
- If you want something bad enough, your enthusiasm can wear people down.

THERE'S MORE TO LIFE THAN MONEY – ESPECIALLY IF YOU'RE RICH

There was a highway location that everyone knew was there and was being bid on. The owner was Mr. Donald a very wealthy man.

Like everyone else, I had met with him. But I think I had better follow up than they did and a better personality. I met with him several times, and I think he liked the idea of the young guy battling the big companies.

After several months of meetings, he chose me over all the others. Was it the money I offered? Hardly, I am sure I was not a high bidder. We just had a good relationship, and he valued that more than money.

He died not too long after the sign was built. He was a great guy, and I really sort of missed him.

You must never underestimate the importance of a relationship. People don't have a lot of loyalty to brands anymore – I buy the cheapest Kleenex at the grocery store as well as least expensive toilet paper.

Your best bet at securing a lease is to build a relationship with the landowner. It is more important than money to most people.

🗵 **LESSONS LEARNED:**
- It is always good to build a relationship
- If you have to choose, better to have a good relationship and a lower offer than vice versa.

THIS DEAL IS TOO WEIRD TO BELIEVE

There was a billboard that was empty with a phone number on it. It belonged to the property owner, a used car dealer. I called him and he said he would sell it for $50,000. All he wanted on the ground rent was $1 a year if I would give him $50,000. So I put in the lease a term of 100 years. He didn't flinch, he wanted the $50,000.

Several years later, he called me and wanted to buy it back for $50,000. I told him that it wasn't for sale; we had a bunch of signs and needed every one to cover our overhead. So he offered $70,000. Still, we had no interest; it was a good money-making sign.

Then, we got another call that let the cat out of the bag. It was from Walgreen's. They had the property under contract, but they could not buy it unless they could get the sign removed. So I did what any good American would do -- I stuck it to them. My price: $250,000 cash. They had cardio arrest.

It wasn't too risky a gamble for me, because the sign was a good sign, but there was no way that as a sign it was worth $250,000.

So I sat and waited. They offered $100, 000, then $150,000, but I had no interest.

In the end, as you guessed it, I got $250,000 and they got the sign.

Now that's a return on investment!

☒ LESSONS LEARNED:

- When the opportunity comes to stick it to "the man", do it with gusto

- You can't get it if you don't ask for it

- Sometimes sign deals lead you down weird paths that offer even more benefits.

A BRIEF INTERMISSION

This book is half-way through, and you are probably getting tired.

Let's take a minute to review what you should be learning so far:

Great deals start off as average deals that end up with some luck – greater traffic on the road, a growing community, and more businesses opening nearby. The important thing is to build your economics on average deals which are basically deals that will still be a winner even if you never get a lucky break.

You should shoot for a 20% return on the total investment (debt and equity) on the billboard. If you meet this rule, then you will pay the sign off in about 7 years (assuming a 10% interest rate) and be able to weather a recession once in a while.

Think outside the box at all times. Creativity is a powerful weapon that through history has lead to some of the greatest achievements. And it often favors the underdog who does not have any bureaucracy to convince.

Examples of this theory:

George Washington vs. the British (not fighting in organized lines)

William Wallace vs. the British (using pointy sticks and flaming pitch)

Microsoft (convinced IBM to put its software in computer)

Apple computer (built first PC)

The returns available in billboards are amazing, and the risk is ridiculously low. Flipping leases is one of the greatest business models on earth

OK, now get back to reading!!

Sometimes Nice Guys Do Finish First

I got a call from a guy who owned a shopping center in Dallas on a major freeway. There already was a billboard on this property, but the lease had expired, and the sign company was low-balling the owner and had really made him mad. I never for a moment thought that the guy was serious about signing up with another company – I figured he was just getting ammunition to use to renegotiate the incumbent. But I was as friendly as could be when the guy called, and told him the honest truth about what the location was worth.

Imagine my shock when, weeks later, he asks me to send him a lease. I sent it to him promptly, but I still didn't expect the deal to go anywhere. Then suddenly, it came back to me in the mail signed.

Now, the first real challenge was how to get the permit, since the old sign had the permit, and all the old company had to do was move it over fifty feet and this guy's location would be blocked. So I hatched a plan. I would file for the permit every day and hope that I got in line with my application before the other guy. He would have to file for a demolition permit to remove the sign, and once the demolition permit was approved, the next application in line would win. It was kind of like a million people calling in to a radio show to see who was caller number 50. That's about the best plan I could come up with.

Then I got a break. The city accidentally gave the permit to me without checking to see that there was another sign already there. I knew they would catch this mistake quickly, so there was only one thing to do – put the foundation for the sign in immediately. Once the foundation was in, it would be impossible to rescind my permit since construction had already begun. Of course, we didn't have any plans to work from – the key was to get something in quickly and figure it out later.

Once the foundation went in, all heck broke loose. The incumbent company didn't know what was going on until we put in the foundation. They immediately threatened to sue me. So I threatened to counter sue for tortuous interference of business. Their attorney told them they had no case, and that I did, so they dropped the whole idea.

Instead, they arranged to meet me at a hotel lobby with another offer. The offer was $50,000 cash to walk away form the deal. They would match the ground rent to the owner that I had offered. I told them I'd take the deal if they gave me $50,000 and one of their signs, so that I still had a sign to show for my trouble. This was a ridiculous request, but they were clearly over a barrel, since this sign location was an integral part of their rotary program.

So for about 20 hours of work, both phone and typing, I receive $50,000 cash and a billboard worth another $50,000. Only in the billboard business!

☒ LESSONS LEARNED FORM THIS DEAL:

- Be easy to buy from. It works two ways: 1) Being nice to the landowner when I thought he was wasting my time. 2) Being nice to the incumbent and listening to their proposal and working with them on it.

- Carpe diem on permits.

ANOTHER CITY COUNCIL VICTORY

I went to a city, more like a small town, on a major highway. They didn't allow signs. So, of course, I asked to appear before the city council. My sales pitch was that billboards offered valuable information to motorists, and would make the town look more "big city" and offer some property tax income for the town.

As always, I went back meeting after meeting, to build up that guilt feeling on the council. There were always two or three people who hated the idea and killed it. But one time none of them showed up. It was sheer luck. The council voted and in their absence, it passed.

I built the sign and it looked just as promised. I rented to a bank and a car dealer and I delivered all my promises.

So, I went back for another one. And, now that they were familiar with my work, they agreed again.

Those signs cost about $30,000 each to build, and sold for about $60,000 each in 1996.

☒   *LESSONS LEARNED:*

- City council appearances are a great, free idea to create value.

- By going to meetings enough, you make them feel guilty over time, and improve your odds of winning.

- If something works, keep trying until it stops working.

Flipping Leases Beats Flipping Burgers

In 1984, I so totally dominated the market on Interstate 35 that I decided to cull out the weaker locations I had just signed up and sell them off. I figured it would give me some quick cash to be used as the down payment on building the rest.

So, I put together a package of four leases and permits, which offered fairly weak visibility. I sent the package to all of my competitors, and several made bids. I played them off against each other, and one showed to be the clear winner.

And look at the results. I had only about $150 in each lease and permit (permit fees). I got $20,000 for each lease and permit, for a total of $80,000. And that was in 1984 dollars!

Who ever heard of an industry where you could sell your garbage for nearly six digits? Flipping leases is an amazingly profitable hobby or career. In fact, sometimes there's more money in flipping leases than there is in taking all the risk of building the unit. As someone once told me "nobody ever went bankrupt taking a profit".

☒   *LESSONS LEARNED:*

- Nothing on earth offers the sheer return on your time as flipping leases.

- You could set up a program to flip your weak leases to pay for the good ones you build as a business model.

- You should carefully compare the returns to selling the lease and permit versus building the unit – you may be better off flipping it.

Now This Was A Strange Deal

There was a 14' x 48' monopole billboard structure on a trucking company, advertising their trucking company. Screwing around in the city records for signs, I found that this billboard had a non-premise permit rather than a premise permit, which meant it, could legally advertise anything.

So, I went to the owner and they told me they were happy with being on their own sign. So, I offered to build them an identical sign for their business at the other end of the property and then pay them groundrent monthly for the current sign structure.

Of course, this made logical sense, and they signed up my deal.

☒ *LESSONS LEARNED:*

- There are billboards out there that everyone assumes are premise signs that really have non-premise permits. Check the old signs out – you may get lucky!

The Best Investment of an Evening You Could Make

There was a small town outside Dallas that had great highway frontage in a desirable, growing area. But they did not allow billboards.

So I decided to talk to the city council and make a proposal:

I would build two "welcome to _____" signs, one at each end of town if they would give me the permits for three monopole structures.

The city council met at night every month in a metal building where the town fire trucks were parked. They were a group of mostly blue-collar workers and farmers, and a nicer bunch of guys you never did meet. When I first approached them with the proposal, they weren't really excited about it since nobody likes billboards. But every month, there I was to pitch them again on it. Over time I became a regular fixture at the council meetings. But what I was really doing was putting a guilt trip on everyone that I would waste my evening every month by going to the council meetings.

One night, the council seemed strangely more interested in my proposal. I think they felt sorry for me. They asked me more detailed questions like what size the signs would be and how long they would take to build.

Several meetings later, they voted and approved my proposal.

I built the three billboards and the two premise signs for the town. I never had any more problems with the signs, and they leased up right away. When I sold them in 1996, they brought $240,000, a nice return on a $90,000 investment.

☒ **LESSONS LEARNED:**

- Investing time in a worthwhile project is a reasonable risk, and sometimes pays off handsomely.

- Never give up

- If you meet with someone long enough, they will feel guilty if they don't give you something in return.

ANOTHER BIG COMPANY LACK OF VISION

I got a call from a big company that they had a "dog" sign for sale. Real cheap, about $5,000.

As always, it was a sign that had been vacant for about two years. I drove it, and immediately liked it. Of course, I bought it before I had even seen it, since at that price; the sign would be worth more than $5,000 as scrap.

It was a major surface street in a market in Ft. Worth that had seen better days, it was clearly going downhill. But it was a nice big 10'6" x 36' monopole, and I knew from experience that the big company sales people had put in virtually no effort to rent it.

I followed the steps to rent it as outlined in my book "Big Profit from Big Signs". The big company had only focused on big time advertisers. They never even bothered to contact the small, local businesses that were located up and down the street.

I did a mass-mailing to these small businesses, and immediately had enough demand to fill both sides of the sign. Let's do the math together. I spent $5,000 for the sign. I rented the sign faces for $400 per month each, and the ground rent was $200 per month. What that equals is about a 100% return per year on my investment.

☒ LESSONS LEARNED:

- Big companies can make stupid decisions.

- You can always rent the sign if you use my approach and reach several categories of advertisers with a "what would you give me" spin to it.

- Stay close to the big companies so you can buy their "dogs".

A Simple, Profitable Billboard Transaction

One market that I dominated was Highway 80 east of Dallas. I built the first steel monopole on this highway, and kept building more because they offered stable economics and the promise of growth in the future.

Highway 80 is an old highway that was greatly reduced by the construction of a parallel interstate highway. When it lost its interstate ranking, nobody seemed to care much about it. But I was attracted to the large number of businesses that were left in place when the interstate reduced the number of cars. I figured that these businesses would still want to reach the traffic, even if it was reduced. And, due to the traffic reduction and general lack of interest, the ground rents would be cheap. This market proved to be the perfect example of building your business around one niche market. I built so many signs on this highway over time, that it could have been a free-standing company on its own.

My economics were simple. The ground rent was $200 per month. The signs rented for $500 per month per face. The signs cost $30,000 to build each. After expenses and a conservative degree of vacancy, it was a 20% cap rate. With 20% down and 10% interest rates, my cash-on-cash return was about 40%.

Equally important, my guess on growth proved correct. As Dallas spread farther and farther out in its suburbs, new houses started sprouting up all over the place, and the rents and number of advertisers became even stronger. All together, I owned about 40 faces in this finite market, and had a virtual monopoly, except for some old wooden signs. And my efficiencies were enormous -- I used the same prospect lists to find advertisers for every sign, and totally controlled the rent levels.

I sold these signs as a group in 1996 for a profit of about $20,000 per sign, or $600,000 collectively. And that was on a capital investment of $120,000, which generated 40% per year cash-on-cash until it was sold.

⊠ LESSONS LEARNED:

- If you come upon a profitable niche, keep adding and exploiting it.

- There are some big efficiencies if you have a tight cluster of desirable signs.

- A lot of big companies ignore markets for surface reasons without really thinking it through.

A SLEEPY MARKET WITH SOLID NUMBERS

It was on an antique shop trip with my wife that I discovered a sleepy little niche south of Ft. Worth. I think it again serves as a perfect example of how you can build a whole business around one finite niche.

The market was a small town about 30 miles south of Ft. Worth, Texas. It was a real old town that had seen its best days in the 1920's. But it still had a large infrastructure of family businesses from the roaring 20's -- pizza shops, restaurants, lawyers, doctors, clothing stores, car dealers. And all of these little advertisers would like a billboard.

I built the first steel monopole in this market. And I was frankly worried; since I was not sure the market could accept something new. I got a ground lease of $100 per month and built a 12' x 24' monopole structure (I built it that size so I could sell it to a big company some day as a 30-sheet poster unit). I did my regular drill of mass mailings and phoning all of the prime prospects. I priced the ad faces real low at $300 per month. And it worked. In no time, I had both faces rented for $300 per month each.

I built the sign cheap for $15,000. So I had total revenue of $7,200 per year, less $1,200 ground rent and about $2,000 in expenses, so I had achieved a better than 20% return on the $15,000 to build it.

Apparently, nobody else cared about this market, so I kept building new signs as soon as I leased the old ones. Of course I tied up all of the legal locations upfront, knowing I could sell the leases off if I had to.

I built about 10 signs in this market, and that would have been nice little business in its own right. I sold them off in 1996 for a huge gain -- a gain that anyone could have had if they had just put in a little vision.

☒ *LESSONS LEARNED:*

- Think outside the box
- If you find a niche, relentlessly exploit it.
- Sometimes you can find neat deals a little bit outside the normal geography of the city (never forget that Wal-Mart started out in small towns).

A SIGN THAT LIVED MANY LIVES AND ALL PROFITABILITY

This story is about a sign that began as a wooden telephone pole-type structure probably back in the 1960's. I saw it abandoned alongside of a major surface street. I contacted the property owner, and found that the structure and permit belonged to them, having obtained it from the billboard company when they abandoned the structure in the early 1980's.

I offered to start paying ground rent immediately, and they gave me the sign. The ground rent was $1,500 per year, and the sign faces rented for $300 per month each. After expenses, the sign made about $4,000 per year on an investment of about $1,000.

I ran the sign in this manner for many years. During that time, the road gained more traffic, and new subdivisions started popping up around it. I thought that it could be put to a higher and better use. So I used my permit to reconstruct a new monopole sign structure. Additionally, to get the city part of the permit, I had to get a variance. And the city was totally psyched on getting rid of the wooden sign in favor of a new monopole. So effectively I used the ugliness of the sign as blackmail to get the new pretty sign.

The economics on this new sign worked equally well, and I sold it in 1996 for a profit of about $40,000.

☒ LESSONS LEARNED:

- There is a lot of profitability in reconditioning old wooden signs.

- Always stay abreast of market developments so you can see new opportunities with old signs.

- Often you can use an ugly sign as a negotiating tool to get a permit for a bigger, more valuable sign.

AN ABANDONED BILLBOARD GETS A NEW LIFE

There was a billboard on the edge of downtown Dallas that had been out of use for many, many years. It was a steel I-beam structure with 14' x 48' faces, so I was shocked that nobody seemed to care much about it, particularly since it had good visibility from an Interstate highway.

I found the owner of the sign, and that might explain the reluctance of billboard guys to try to take it over -- it was owned by the "by-the-hour" motel underneath the sign. I had to take a bodyguard to the meeting (my art director) to make sure that I would make it back to the office. The motel was seemingly run by the mob, as it had thugs lining the upper balconies, spaced evenly about every 20 feet.

I offered $400 per month ground rent if they would sell me the sign for $1. Without even negotiating, they signed my paperwork.

This sign's existence was a good case model for the billboard ordinances at that time. Sign permits in Dallas do not require, or at least back then didn't, annual renewal. Once the sign is built, the permit is permanent unless you abandon the sign for a certain length of time. Since the sign still had 30 year old ads on it, it didn't really look abandoned. But I had to file to get the electricity turned back on for the lights, which triggered the billboard department of city hall. They green-tagged me, and I was ready to rent space.

When you go to rent space on a billboard that has been seen with the same ads for many years, it is easy for the advertiser to identify the sign in their mind. The ads rented quickly to local businesses, who knew it as the Earl White's Review sign (Earl White apparently had a big band -- guess that helps date when the ads were painted).

The faces rented for $600 per month each, for a total of $1,200 per month of revenue. Expenses were about $700 per month, for a net income of $6,000 per year. It only cost about $3,000 to put the sign back in service, so the return was about 200% per year.

When I sold the sign in 1996, it was treated as an important 14' x 48' sign on a major freeway near downtown, and brought about $80,000. This was a huge return on $3,000.

I still see signs like this anywhere I go in the U.S. -- there's probably at least one in your market.

⊠ **LESSONS LEARNED:**

- Abandoned signs can be enormously lucrative to re-open.

- Think outside the box, especially concerning scary meetings. Take along a friend, or even hire an off-duty policeman if you need to. Although the setting was dangerous, the landowners were perfectly fine in person.

PIONEERING A BLIGHTED MARKET WITH HIGH TRAFFIC VOLUME

South Dallas has always had a bad reputation. Although it is the prettiest part of the city, it has low demographics and some dangerous pockets. So, consequently, nobody put a lot of effort into the billboard business down there.

I was fascinated that there were available billboard locations on a highway with a 100,000+ per day traffic count. So I started typing up locations and permits. I found the pickings abundant, and what amazed me was that my neighbors were some of the biggest billboard companies in the U.S., who surely knew these legal locations were there, but simply passed on them.

I knew that to create maximum value, I would need to build 14' x 48' monopoles, but the economics weren't very strong. The ground leases were about $400 per month, but to local businesses in that market, the going rate was only about $500 per month per face. That didn't leave much cash to pay the debt service. So I came up with a wild idea.

I went to the biggest competitor, who had a very mature rotary billboard program. Under a rotary, the ad moves to a new sign every 90 days. I had noticed that the rotary program was full in this market, despite its low demographics.

I proposed to sublease the constructed units to their rotary program at the low, low rate of only $1,000 per month per structure ($500 per face). Rotary signs rented for $3,000 per month back then. My strategy was that I could make the note payment if I had no other expenses (lights or painting) and 100% occupancy with no vacancy.

To my amazement, they agreed to the deal, and signed up for five years per structure. My loans were only five years in amortization, so what it meant was that they would give me back the billboards in five years free and clear.

This program was a huge hit for me. The bank loved the five year commitment. I loved the absence of risk and effort. And they seemed to like having the signs in their rotary.

And why had they not just built the signs themselves? It was classic big company. The real estate guys figured if they ever needed another sign, they would just go get the lease at that time. And the guys who built them didn't want to commit the capital out of their budget. And nobody listened to the sale department.

☒ *LESSONS LEARNED:*

- Big companies do stupid stuff
- High traffic highways can make up for almost any demographic problem
- Subleasing ad space can be a winner.

HONESTY IS THE BEST POLICY -- IF IT GETS YOUR LEASE SIGNED

There was a great 14' x 48' major interstate location in Dallas that had never been built on because the owner seemingly had no interest in a billboard.

I wrote the guy a letter and, like everybody else, got no response. I called, and the secretary said he had no interest. So I decided to give it one more shot and do some office sitting. I drove to the guy's office and asked to see him. The secretary said he had no interest, but I asked to see him just the same and, not knowing what to say, let me sit in the reception room. I took along some paperwork and magazines in my briefcase, because these types of expeditions take a lot of time. I got there at 10 a.m. At 5 p.m., when the office is shutting down for the day, the guy agrees to see me for one minute.

The owner was a big developer, and had no time for B.S., so sensing I had only about one minute to impress him, I laid out the business plan quick. He had a legal sign location. They are rare. It would be a shame to waste it. I knew he had tons of money, but couldn't he give the $500 per month ground rent to a charity, or a family member as a gift. I had photos of where the sign would go and what it would look like. And my straight forward approach must have triggered something in his past from when he started out as a developer. He cut me off and said "Kid, I've got the picture already, if you really want the location that bad, then what the hell". I left my lease with him and went home.

Weeks passed, and I never heard from him. Then, suddenly, my lease arrived in the mail with a post-it note that said "good luck". I built the sign and never saw the guy again.

Any sign on a major interstate inside the city limits is a big winner and this sign was no exception. It rented for $800 per face, and made about a 20% return on investment.

I found out years later that they guy had died not long after our meeting. Perhaps, the fact that he was getting so old and losing enthusiasm for what he did, made my enthusiasm that much more attractive.

☒ LESSONS LEARNED:

- Amazing results can come of face-to-face meetings.
- Office sitting can be very lucrative, because it can make things happen.

I BRAVE THE PROJECTS AND BRING HOME A BILLBOARD LEASE - BARELY

There was a billboard location I was interested in and I found the owner. It was a funeral home in the projects. I called the owner of the funeral home up and she said she would be happy to meet with me, but only at the funeral home. It seemed that she also lived there. She was elderly and never really left the place. So I set up a meeting.

When I got there I was absolutely too afraid to get out of the car. Here I was, in a suit, surrounded by gangs and street people. But I really wanted that lease. So I convinced myself that it wasn't really as bad as it looked. So I opened the door, and the whole crowd started walking toward me, so I jumped back in my car and took off around the block.

I had arrived a little early, so I thought I would try again. This time waiting until the crowd had dispersed. So when things got real calm, I pulled in again and got out of the car. This time, before I could turn around again, a street person accosted me, demanding money, and I saw several more approaching. So I jumped back in the car and took off. This time I was convinced that I should quit. No lease was worth getting killed over. So I started to drive back to the office. Then, like a scene out of the Magnificent Seven, I turned around again, convinced that no low-life people from the projects were going to keep me from my billboard location. So I parked for a third time and, giving my best "Godfather" imitation, walked briskly to the door with the street people, and gang members behind me.

It took only about thirty minutes to finalize the lease. But I was terrified about how I would get back to my car alive, or if my car was even still there, or still had tires. Once the lease was signed and in my briefcase, I told the woman my fear in getting back to my car. So she had an embalmer walk me back and, since everyone knew him, they didn't bother me. And the car was still there too.

The sign was a solid performer and sold for a $40,000 profit years later.

☒ *LESSONS LEARNED:*

- There are billboard locations that have not been signed up because people are too afraid to go to the meeting. Don't be as stupid as I was. Hire a security guard, if you have to, but find some way to get to that meeting. Remember, you only have to meet once.

A Different Way To Get A Location -- Riskier But More Profitable

I had been looking for sign locations to add to my collection on Interstate 35 south of Dallas. One location had all the right elements; correct spacing, correct zoning. Everything but a willing landowner.

After bugging the guy about leasing 9 square feet of ground space out of his 1 acre tract, he instead suddenly offered to sell it to me for $25,000. This was an unusual occurrence. Seldom did a landowner offer to sell me their land, and at such a low dollar figure (actually it was quite high as land sold for only about $10,000 per acre in this market, so really it was 2.5 times market).

Now, buying a piece of land to build a billboard is normally the tail wagging the dog. But in this case, there is a methodology to make it a winning idea.

I tied up the land at the $25,000 and filed for my billboard permit. Meanwhile, I found a commercial broker who promised that he could sell the land prior to closing for at least $15,000, with my company keeping a perpetual easement to have a billboard on the land. To summarize, I was going to have a permanent billboard ocation at a cost of only $10,000 (roughly five times my annual proposed ground rent).

I got my permit, but the real pressure was on getting the land sold off prior to closing, so that I only had to come up with $10,000. As with most brokers, this guy could not deliver on his promise, and closing was approaching with no buyer in hand. So I was feverishly phoning every sign contractor in northern Texas, looking for a cheap monopole that I could use to offset the land cost. In a miracle, I found a used structure that had just been taken down for $15,000 installed. That meant that I needed a loan of $40,000 to cover the land and billboard.

The deal offered the bank two unusual benefits: a permanent sign location with no risk of removal and $0 ground rent. Equally important was the fact that it was a real estate deal -- banks love real estate deals. So I got my loan, closed on the tract and built my sign. I had totally misjudged the world of land sales, however, and it took about a year to re-sell the land, and at less then we budgeted. However, in the interim they announced a new development in the area and I beat my revenue budget to make up for it.

☒ LESSONS LEARNED:

- In the right circumstances, it is a great idea to buy the land under the sign rather than build it.

- Never give up. It was my scramble to find a cheap structure that made the loan possible.

- Always scramble early on. If I had waited until the last minute on any part of this deal, it would have died.

I Buy Land Again

After my foray on Interstate 35, I decided to try it again on a landowner who would not lease me his land for a sign spot, and had a fairly small tract.

It was an old house on Interstate 45 that had commercial zoning, despite being in a residential neighborhood. If you look closely at your zoning maps, you will see that sometimes a few houses will end up as commercial zoning when there is a freeway frontage involved.

The guy was more than happy to sell me his run-down rental house in the bad part of town for $45,000. Like before, the plan was to buy the house, build the billboard, re-sell the house and keep a permanent easement for the sign (I later called this concept "buy/trim/flip").

Before I could build the billboard, I sold the whole deal to another billboard company to hedge my risk. I am always interested in flipping a deal to someone else at the right price. I walked away with about $20,000 in profits.

The other company did just as I had figured; they built the sign and re-sold the house.

☒ *LESSONS LEARNED:*

- In the right circumstances, buying the land instead of leasing it is a great plan.

- Flipping leases and permits is a fantastic way to make money with no risk.

I Fight City Hall and Win

I found a billboard location, again on Interstate 45, that had all the correct criteria -- right zoning, right spacing, and an agreeable landowner. I signed up a lease and applied for a permit.

My permit was turned down. The inspector ruled that the sign on another surface street, but visible from the highway, made my spot the wrong spacing from the next sign. I knew this interpretation was wrong, because that sign was not designed to be seen from the highway -- it was only 12' x 24' and you could not even make out what was on it!

I argued with the inspector, but he was firm in his position. I asked to talk to his boss, but he had already back-stabbed me with the boss, so they would not even meet with me. So I did a first in my career, I hired an attorney to get some action. I showed the attorney all of the subtle nuances of the laws, and photos of the sign in question.

Whenever an attorney calls city hall, people get extremely serious or at least pretend to be, since the city does not like litigation. Obviously, my case was tiny compared with normal complaints, but then again the whole goal of the city staff is to keep their jobs and live for the weekend.

Without even a meeting with my attorney, but just based on phone calls, the inspector was told to go ahead and give me the permit.

The sign cost about $35,000 to build, and sold for $80,000 in 1996.

Had I not stood up to city hall, I would have been $45,000 poorer and carrying a grudge.

☒ LESSONS LEARNED:

- If you know you are in the right, don't be afraid to tackle city hall. But make sure you know you are in the right. When you take on city hall, you burn a lot of bridges and you don't want to do that for anything less than a 100% sure thing.

- If you do not get satisfaction at city hall, hire an attorney. Cities, for some reason, don't think you're serious unless you invest some money in an attorney.

I Fight City Hall Again -- Accidentally -- And Win Again

I had spent some time trying to find a legal location on Highway 67 south of Dallas. The location I finally leased was right across from the airport, next to McDonalds.

I got my sign lease and permit and then shortly thereafter I got a letter from City Hall announcing that they were going to expand the airport, and my permit was hereby revoked.

I knew this case was in need of an attorney, so I presented all of my stuff to the attorney who had won against city hall before. His position was that my sign lease and permit had value, and they would have to compensate me through condemnation and not just revoke my permit. They had damaged me and I deserved just compensation.

He sent the city a demand letter, and a new wrinkle popped up. They had quietly already bought the McDonalds and land around me, and they wanted to get that airport expansion going right now. They did not have time for a lawsuit or a condemnation hearing. This was their weak spot -- time.

To our amazement, they suddenly made their weirdest counter-offer in billboard history. They would allow me to move my sign location anywhere I wanted on Highway 67, even if it did not meet the spacing requirements. There was a spot that was about 500' south of my location, but it was totally illegal. But they agreed to give me a new permit anyway. And this new location was at a much lover ground lease cost.

In the end, I got my billboard at a new location that did not in any way meet the city's spacing requirement, and reduced my ground lease by about 50%

☒ *LESSONS LEARNED:*

- Don't be afraid to take on city hall if you know you have a good case.

- Always hire an attorney when fighting city hall -- that is the trigger for them to take you seriously

- Be negotiable. Had I held out for condemnation damages, rather than move my sign location, I might have gotten nothing, plus I would have had to risk huge legal fees.

Cold Calling Bank Repo Departments Finally Pays off

I had started a routine of calling all bank repo departments to see if they had any repossessed billboards to sell. I first sent them a form letter concerning my interest, and then I would call all of them at least once per month to touch base.

Initially, the project had no success at all. Then, about six months into the practice, I got a break. The loan officer said he did have a billboard for sale, and would take about $10,000 for it. I had never seen it, but it was a monopole, and I figured that any monopole would be worth, including lights and panels, at least that much in scrap.

So I committed to buy the sign without seeing it first (of course, after seeing it I could have refused to pay, and the only damage would have been my loss of a relationship with that bank).

When I drove out to see the sign, I was amazed. I had just committed to buy a new 14' x 48' monopole with all lights and panels. So I then began to worry that someone inside the bank would realize that this was a huge mistake, and not go forward with it. So I expedited closing in every way I could, and the sign was mine.

The next issue was the ground lease. The lease had been cancelled due to non-payment of the rent. However, I had paid so little for the sign that I could "pay-off" the landowner to start a new lease with me, to the tune of about $2,000. The new lease was $300 per month.

The sign rented quickly for $600 per side, and the net income on the $12,000 investment was $8,000 per year, or a 67% return on investment. I held the sign for six years, and then sold it in 1996 for about $70,000.

☒ LESSONS LEARNED:

- Banks can make stupid errors. The bank officer didn't know anything about billboard valuations, and didn't try to learn.

- When someone makes a mistake, rush to close before they figure it out.

- Never give up. If I had given up calling on banks I would have never found this deal

- When someone offers you a great deal, take it sight unseen. You can always back out, but if you act undecided, they may call somebody else and get a bidding war going.

A Little Niche

While renting a billboard I owned on I-35 in Ft. Worth, I came across an RV dealer that did a fairly large sales volume, and spent a large amount of money on a billboard program.

He didn't want the sign I had near his sales lot, but he did want a location on a lesser traveled farm-to-market road that I had always considered too rural. However, he was willing to pay about $400 per month for a billboard there on a three year lease.

So I started looking at locations, and of course there were plenty of options. So I found one that offered curve-in-the-road exposure at a low ground rent. But what really worried me was that there were so many other legal locations, what would stop someone else from flooding the market with signs?

The only security I had was two fold 1) I had better visibility and lower ground rent than theirs would be, so I had some competitive advantage and 2) I had a three year lease to give me time to pay down some significant debt.

The other problem was that I did not want to spend much on the structure. Since I knew this location would not be of value down the road, as it was too rural, I bought a cheap 10' x 30' that had been torn down (I knew that, in a pinch, a big company could arguably modify that size into a 12' x 24' 30-sheet poster panel)

I rented the other side for $250 per month, and so I had $650 in revenue and about $250 per month in expense, for a net of $4,800 per year.

The structure cost about $12,000 to build, so I had a very attractive 40% return on investment. Most importantly, when the three years lease expired, I would only owe next to nothing on the structure, and I could move it to another location if I could not sell the ad space.

☒ LESSONS LEARNED:

- Building a sign for an advertiser's unique desires can be profitable if they will sign a lease long enough to virtually pay-off your debt.

- When building a sign in a market ripe with unused locations, shop around and get a great one, so that you will have some type of advantage over the other guy.

I SUBLEASE ONE SIDE OF A FUEL STOP SIGN

This is not one of my best deals, or even close. But I wanted to include it because it's an opportunity that I don't want you to miss out on, and I see them all the time.

There was a truck "fuel stop" on an Interstate Highway at a certain exit. Years ago, they had built their own billboard about 1 mile before their exit. But they were stuck with one side of their sign that was facing the wrong direction for their purpose. So they put a generic ad on it for their fuel stop, but it clearly had no purpose other than to hide the backside of the sign they needed.

I went to them and offered to lease it from them for $50 per month. The rationale was that they could use that money to do some other form of promotion that would actually benefit them (yellow page, small print ad, sponsor a little league team, etc.)

They had no problem with it, and the economics worked for me, too. I rented the face for $350 per month to a business heading in the other direction, and the economics, while in no way stunning, were pretty creative. My total cost was $50 for the sign, plus electric and paint. So my net was about $200 per month for almost no time, effort or risk.

When you are starting your billboard company, a quick $200 per month of cash flow is extremely important.

☒ *LESSONS LEARNED:*

- There are many opportunities for creating monthly cash flow incomes if you think outside the box.

- Subleasing an underutilized sign structure is a good way to make money without any capital investment.

I Buy Another Dog Sign From A Big Company, And Then Maximize Its Yeild

A big company offered my favorite deal -- I could buy one of their "dog" signs for $2,000. This was a structure on a fairly well-traveled surface street. But it did have issues. But these were issues I could improve upon.

The structure was made up of two side-by-side 12'x 24' poster units, held up by many steel poles. I immediately changed this face to one large 14' x 48'. Additionally, it had no ads on the back side, so I put a 14' x 48' on that side too. I also added lights to the structure -- it had been a non-lighted unit.

It turned out that the best market for the main face on the sign was a group of topless bars down the street. They had never advertised on it because it was not lighted at night, which was their peak time.

So I rented it quickly, and for about $700 per month. The other side was trickier, because it had a bad obstruction to about 30% of the sign from that canopy of a gas station. So I designed an advertising design that only utilized the upper two-thirds of the sign, and left the blocked portion blank. Kind of a 9' x 48' ad face. I got it rented for $400 per month.

So, I had revenue of $1,100 per month and costs of only $200 ground rent plus lights and paint, for a net of $8,000 per year. It cost me about $5,000 to re-work the sign, so the return was about 100% per year on investment.

☒ *LESSONS LEARNED:*

- Stay in close contact with big companies so that you can buy these dog signs.

- Think outside the box at all times

- Upgrade every unit to its highest and best use. In this case, had the big company installed lights on the unit, it would have never been a dog.

I FIND AN AMAZING OVERSIGHT BY A COMPETITOR

While I was building billboards on I-35 south of Dallas, I was intrigued by the tiny sign that held a permit to build a 14' x 48'.

What had happened was that a company that specialized in 8-sheet signs, 5' x 10' in size, had leased ground and built a unit on the highway to add to the list of dots in their 8-sheet inventory. It was a gross misuse of space, since you could hardly see the tiny 8-sheet face from the highway.

I knew that they would never sell it to me, but that the property owner couldn't be getting much from this tiny sign. I talked to the owner and they were only getting $500 per year, and the lease was on month-to-month. When I told them that I could pay $300 per month they were ready to do whatever I wanted. So I told them to call the 8-sheet guy and offer to buy the sign, or otherwise ask him to remove it. My fear was that he would move it next door and block my ability to get a permit. My bet was correct and the 8-sheet guy offered to sell it to the landowner for $2,000 (a really high price for an 8-sheet). I gave him the $2,000 and he deeded it to me for $1. I then filed a demolition permit and a new permit application.

This was the equivalent to paying $2,000 for a lease and permit. At a time when people flipped leases for $20,000 or more, this was a real bargain.

I built the sign, and it made about $10,000 net income per year.

☒ **LESSONS LEARNED:**

- When you see an underutilized sign location, and it can be made into something better, try to buy or take control of it.

- Always think outside the box. The 8-sheet guy never even saw this opportunity, or he could have had it for free.

I WINE AND DINE MY WAY INTO A 14′ X 48′ FREEWAY LOCATION

This is a story of persistence and the weird situations that landowners may put you into to get a lease.

The location in questions was on Interstate 35 in Dallas. It had great visibility in one direction and fair in the other, and I was ready to pay $400 per month for it. But the landowner would not sign my lease. He was indifferent, and no matter what I did he seemed to have no sense of urgency at all.

It turned out that he had a partner on the land, and he needed his approval too. But these guys never got together, so clearly it would take months, or years, before the deal would be put together. So I offered to take them both out to dinner at the restaurant of their choice if they would talk about the billboard. Always a sucker for a free dinner, they agreed to the unusual offer.

They picked what, at the time, as Dallas's most expensive restaurant. And they ordered the most expensive stuff on the menu. Lobster, crab, shrimp, whatever they could find. When the bill came, they had stuck me with a $300 tab. The only good news was that they felt guilty, and felt like they owed me something, which happened to be a billboard lease.

We signed up the lease before we left the table, about 50% out of guilt and pity.

I built the sign and it made about $10,000 per year for me.

☒ LESSONS LEARNED:

- If I had not come up with the dinner concept, this deal would never have happened.

- It never hurts to build up a guilt complex for the landowner or the city council, or anyone you want something from. That guilt is worth every penny it costs.

I TAKE A CITY ORDINANCE AND WORK BACKWARDS

This sign deal was not that impressive; except that it illustrates an important concept I want you to think about.

There was a city east of Dallas that was very desirable, with extremely impressive demographics. But as with most nice cities, they didn't want billboards. However, there was a loophole in their city ordinance.

Many cities do not outright ban signs, but instead insert criteria so difficult that theoretically will make it impossible to build signs. However, in this cities case, they did allow a 5' x 10' (8-sheet sized) billboard in a certain zoning that did exist in only one spot in the town. And this one spot was on the way to school, so everyone in the town drove past it every day.

The city just about died when I turned in my sign application. But they had no choice but to give me the permit. Before I could even build it, I flipped it for $15,000 to a big 8 sheet operator who wanted it in his inventory.

☒ *LESSONS LEARNED:*

- There is good money in seeing what a desirable town does allow in the world of billboards, and then building that product, rather than giving up because they do not allow traditional billboard products

- Never give up. Always keep looking for the loophole.

BONUS CHAPTER: HOW TO MITIGATE RISK IN THE BILLBOARD INDUSTRY

In a decade and a half of owning over 300 billboards, I only lost two locations. And this was despite the existence of a termination provision in my lease in the event of development.

If you are going to make money in the billboard business, you have got to know how to mitigate your risk from the three greatest risks.

Lease Termination And Sign Removal

To mitigate your risk in this area, you must think proactively on the consequences of the land being re-developed. Although your billboard means a lot to you, the property owner is only concerned with maximizing his return from the real estate, and if the opportunity comes up to redevelop the property into a higher and more valuable use, you better believe he is going to do so.

First, consider how high a use the land has currently attained. If it is a garden style office building, or a newer hotel, or a successful shopping center, then development won't usually occur in the future. If it's a run-down strip center, or an abandoned warehouse, then development is probably imminent. If it is raw land, then the future is massively uncertain.

Next, consider what the options are for the land. If you are in a run-down warehouse district, then a run-down warehouse may be for now, its highest and best use. If, however, the neighboring property is a high-rise office building, then you may be in trouble.

The next consideration is if you can locate the sign in the corner of the property such that it will be near to impossible to develop the spot on which it sits. If your sign is in the middle of the property, you have a much greater risk of removal.

Finally, assess how much cash flow the sign will make. If it's immensely high cash flow generating, then you may be able to pay off the sign in a couple years, and your risk is reduced. If it is a low-dollar sign, it may take five to seven years to pay off -- maybe longer -- and your risk is much greater.

Now comes the hard part: putting these factors together and coming up with a decision. Nobody ever made money building a billboard and tearing it down a year later. For you to risk money and time and effort and worry on this sign, it must be what appears to be a lifetime commitment. I would never build a sign that might have only a short future, except when it was so profitable that I would have my money back in 12 to 24 months.

If your deal is on raw land in a growing desirable area and your sign is right in the middle of the tract, then that's too risky a deal for me (unless it makes a 50% per year return or greater). If the deal is too risky, I would flip the lease and permit to another player. That's just good business.

I have never passed on a deal, and/or flipped the lease, and regretted it. Every time I have done it, I have seen a few years later the sign I could have built torn down. Boy was I glad that wasn't me.

The only two signs I ever lost, I would have been fine on had I followed my own advice here. My intuition was that they had a very short future, but I so wanted them in my portfolio that I foolishly kept them anyway. What an idiot.

If you ever lose a sign, here's what to do:

- Don't panic. Don't jump out the window upon receiving the termination letter. Think calmly.
- Set up a meeting with the landowner. Propose that he:
    - A. Change his mind
    - B. Delay removal for a while so that you can line up a spot to move it too.
    - Offer to advertise his development on the sign if he will do either (A) or (B)
- Offer to sell it to him for what you have in it, so he can use it for a premise sign
- Find an alternative location to move it to. If you can pull this off, then you will only be out the cost of moving the sign and the crisis is partially averted.
- Learn from your mistake and never make it again.

Wind Damage

If you are in an area of the U.S. where wind damage is likely (and who isn't) you need to have a plan in place to hedge your risks.

First, develop a list of all neighboring businesses (preferably 24 hour) that can see your sign from their window. In the event of a storm, you can call these people to see if you have any visible damage. If you do, you can take proactive measures immediately to stem your losses (pick up your vinyl's and panels for instance)

Annually, have your sign structures checked for welding issues, loose head bolts, etc. This type of proactive behavior may save you form a catastrophic loss.

Don't buy signs that are extremely dangerous; that's first and foremost. If you have a billboard opportunity on the beach in a hurricane zone, reconsider what you are doing. I passed on some first-class billboard in Galveston, Texas once, and when the hurricane hit, boy was I glad. If the spot looks risky, flip the lease and move on.

Vacancy

You can mitigate your risk of vacancy. It's a lot of work, but well worth the effort.

First, always start re-renting a billboard at least 60 days from when the ad expires. Never start actively renting it once the ad expires. That is financial suicide.

Secondly, as discussed in my other book "Big Profits from Big Signs" you set up a series of temporary "pre-emptible" advertisements that can be freely put on vacant faces until you can find a better paying renter. These pre-emptible ads are in two groups:

- Advertisers who advertise generically in the market and would like a low cost situation where they pay for every 30 days they are up. If the market rent is $1,000 per month, then they might pay $500.

- Advertisers who do the same thing but pay through barter scrip, through a barter exchange. This means that they will trade you goods and services instead of cash. While cash is always better, it still beats a vacant sign.

Always remember that a vacant sign has big problems:

- It means you have no money coming in.
- It looks really bad to:

- Potential advertisers who worry that nobody wants that sign so why should they.

- Your bank that worries you don't know what you are doing and/or won't be able to pay the mortgage.

Proactively attack the vacancy issue, and be a winner.

The Top Five Deals I Didn't Do And Why I'm Still Glad I Didn't

Three Big Signs in Atlanta, Georgia

A guy had three big 20' x 60' monopole signs for sale on a major highway in Atlanta. The price was huge at the time; about $300,000 for all three. The numbers supported it.

But I was concerned on two issues:

- Too much concentration in one small market. What if there had been a tornado and all three were knocked down? What if the highway had construction work and the traffic declined? What if that part of Atlanta became just no longer attractive to advertisers?

- There were absolutely no controls to trim back vegetation that was clearly going to block the visibility of the signs down the road. All of the trees were on the highway right-of-way, and there was no way you could trim them. What would I do when the trees obscured the ads?

I have never seen this deal since, but I'm glad I passed on it regardless of how it turned out. It was just too big a gamble.

Five signs in Dallas, Texas market on a motel chain

I worked a deal with the owner of a motel chain to put billboards in the parking lots of each of his motels. They all had good highway frontage.

He negotiated the deal around and in the final bidding; I won at the ground rent percentage of 40% of the gross. I really wanted the deal, but I didn't think anyone would buy them from me down the road at such an outrageous percentage. I wasn't even sure I could get a loan on it. And I didn't like having so much exposure with one landowner. It turns out that I was right. The landowner went bankrupt and half the signs got torn down.   Glad I missed that one.

A Whole Billboard Operation in Tulsa, Oklahoma

This deal would have been a winner, but I'm still glad I passed on it.

It was a bundle of major signs in Tulsa. But most of the leases had expired. More importantly, there were a lot of tree obstructions on highway right-of-ways. Even if I renegotiated all the leases, I would be fighting the tree issues forever. Additionally, I didn't like that much exposure in Oklahoma, which has enormous economic cycles of famine.

If I had bought it, I would have made good money with it. But just as likely, I would have gone bankrupt if any of my fears had proven correct.

A Whole Billboard Operation in Oklahoma City, Oklahoma

Just like the Tulsa deal, this was a collection of signs on mostly surfaced streets in Oklahoma City. The locations were average at best, but the price was cheap. All of the units were 30-sheet poster sized (12' x 24'), and were mostly monopoles.

All of the groundless were cancelled due to nonpayment. I talked to a few of the owners, and they refused to even consider a new lease until they received the back rent, which was usually thousands.

I would have taken on the deal except for the fact that the lender did not want to give me an adequate time to fix everything before closing (I needed about 180 days at least.) They wanted someone to close on it now…as is, and gamble that things could be fixed.

I saw the signs years later, and they were still in shambles. My bet is that whoever bought it was unable to renegotiate any of the leases, and let it go back to the bank again.

Three Signs on a Major Freeway with only a Management Fee

A landowner proposed that he would give me 25% of the net if I managed three billboards for him on a major highway in Dallas. He would build them, and my only job was renting and managing them. The catch: He wanted a huge rent for them, well in excess of the market.

25% of gross is O.K., but not that great for renting six faces of billboards. And I knew I would never get that much for them. So I passed.

Some other schmuck took the deal and was unable to deliver advertisers at those prices. Eventually, he dropped the price and rented them. Shortly thereafter, they built a new freeway entrance ramp and obliterated the visibility of one side of each sign. Man, I sure don't miss that deal.

CPSIA information can be obtained
at www.ICGtesting.com
Printed in the USA
LVHW092138100821
695046LV00009B/43